:: San Francisco

A guide to recent architecture

Peter Lloyd
Photographs by Keith Collie

San Francisco

A guide to recent architecture

•••ellipsis KÖNEMANN

•••

All rights reserved. No part of this publication may be reproduced in any form without written permission from the publisher

San Francisco: a guide to recent architecture

CREATED, EDITED AND DESIGNED BY
Ellipsis London Limited
55 Charlotte Road London EC2A 3QT
E MAIL ...@ellipsis.co.uk
www http://www.ellipsis.co.uk/ellipsis
PUBLISHED IN THE UK AND AFRICA BY
Ellipsis London Limited
SERIES EDITOR Tom Neville
EDITOR Annie Bridges
SERIES DESIGN Jonathan Moberly
LAYOUT Pauline Harrison

COPYRIGHT © 1997 Könemann
Verlagsgesellschaft mbH
Bonner Str. 126, D-50968 Köln
PRODUCTION MANAGER Detlev Schaper
PRINTING AND BINDING Sing Cheong
Printing Ltd
Printed in Hong Kong

ISBN 3 89508 643 6 (Könemann)
ISBN 1 899858 07 5 (Ellipsis)

Contents

Introduction

San Francisco must surely be one of the most beautiful cities in the world. Located on a hilly peninsular that separates the Pacific Ocean from the Bay, it is hard to imagine a more favourable site and hard to imagine how the city could be anything but beautiful.

This is, of course, a naive assumption. Builders, developers, planners and architects have the capacity to make anything ugly and it is a capacity that should not be underestimated.

That San Francisco is not ugly is worth celebrating and the way it makes itself beautiful is worth emulating.

The geography is beyond any city planner's control, but other factors are not. What San Francisco offers is a strong sense of place. The bland business area has not encroached too far into the city's residential areas and it is in these that the city finds its strengths. Neighbourhoods are readily identifiable; small shops still manage to survive; individual houses (although often subdivided) predominate; many people who work in the city live in the city; for those who commute, there are a number of public transport options, ranging from the buses and streetcars that criss-cross the city to the BART trains that link the outer suburbs.

San Franciscans often describe their city as a 'friendly' or 'comfortable' place. These are unostentatious but important words. The need for connection between people is both strong and basic and this city seems to meet it. If this reflects itself in an architecture that is more about place-making than object-making, planners and architects should pay attention.

It is no surprise that the 'New Traditionalist' or 'New Urbanist' school of city planning should be strongly represented in San Francisco. The work of Peter Calthorpe and Daniel Solomon has received particular attention, as has Christopher Alexander's intensely humane book *A*

Pattern Language, which originated across the Bay in Berkeley.

It is also no surprise that a deep-seated conservatism should find expression in San Francisco and the dangers of prissy historicism and smug self-congratulation should not be disregarded. Perhaps this is where the city finds its creative tension: in the conflict between the desire to safe-guard the character and history of the place and the need to ensure that San Francisco stays alive, vibrant and new.

One of the most significant new projects in recent years, the New Main Library (page 108) by the New York-based firm of Pei Cobb Freed and Partners together with the local firm of Simon Martin-Vegue Winkelstein Moris exemplifies this conflict. In this case, a very contextual approach has been taken and the new building mirrors many aspects of the old Library that it faces. Unfortunately the New Main Library seems destined to be a building that satisfies no-one (or, at least, agitates many): it is not the exact copy of the old Library that the conservationists wanted, nor is it the unabashedly modern design – in the mould, say, of Norman Foster's Maison Carrée in Nimes – desired by others.

Other important projects, SF MOMA (page 38) and the Yerba Buena complex (pages 24–42), have taken a more straightforwardly modern approach but the debate as to their success is just as heated.

For each of these projects, architects from outside San Francisco have been brought in, but it is to be hoped that local firms, such as the elegant modernists Jim Jennings and Tanner Leddy Maytum and Stacy, and the more quirky Stanley Saitowitz and Kotas/Pantaleoni, will soon be given substantial assignments.

As significant as any individual project or any individual architect, however, is the emphasis placed by political and planning authorities on the building of low-cost housing. These projects enrich not only the lives

San Francisco: a guide to recent architecture

of their residents but of everybody in the city. Architecture does not solve society's problems, but it is at least heartening to see it trying.

Less heartening is the building that has been going on in the Oakland/ Berkely hills since the fire of 1991. When Coop Himmelblau came up with their slogan 'Architecture must burn', they probably never imagined that it would ever be as literally enacted as in Oakland where 3000 homes were destroyed and 22 people killed. But out of the ashes has come, not a brave new world, but the image of a safe old one. To see so many over-blown haciendas and chateaux is a little depressing. Not because they are haciendas and chateaux but rather because so many of them have expanded to their lot lines and left so little space for planting. Surely the pleasure of living in the hills was the pleasure of living in nature. In light of this I suggest an alternative slogan to Coop Himmelbau's: 'Architecture must grow'.

For anybody who is disheartened by the new houses in the hills, one of the owners of a house featured in this book put things into perspective. He said: 'When I drive around the fire zone I think "Isn't it terrible? Three thousand new houses and only a dozen decent ones", but I know that at the same time there is somebody else driving around saying "Isn't this amazing? Three thousand new houses built and only a dozen bad ones".'

This book features rather more than a dozen houses in the fire zone: you can decide whether they are the good ones or the bad.

On this subject, the choice of projects generally is nothing but subjec-tive. No attempt has been made to establish consistent criteria and the book as a whole is ruled by a spirit of contradiction and contrariness. Or so I would like to think. Uniformity does not do a city any good, why should a book be different?

ACKNOWLEDGEMENTS

Thanks are due to all the architects who gave their time so generously, and to Helen Chakerian, Lian Angus and Peter Haffner.
PL December 1996

San Francisco: a guide to recent architecture

Using this book

All the projects are given a map reference taken from one of two Thomas's Guides: the *San Francisco, Alemeda and Contra Costa Counties* edition, which covers San Francisco and the East Bay; and the *Golden Gate Marin County* guide.

For example: the Rincon Center (SF/A/CC SF 3 B3) will be found at coordinates B3 on page 3 in the San Francisco section of the *San Francisco, Alemeda and Contra Costa Counties* guide.

Having said this, one can very easily find most of the projects without reference to anything grander than a standard $3 street map.

PRIVATE HOUSES
Please respect people's privacy: do not try to enter private residences or other buildings where it is stated that there is no access.

South of Market

Rincon Center and Towers

The Rincon Towers have a touch of Gotham about them: their curved glass walls and corniced towers, topped by Loch Ness monster undulations, seem a little too showy for demure San Francisco. Their scale is deceptive and seen in isolation one would expect them to be vast skyscrapers, dwarfing puny neighbours. In reality they aren't and don't – and more's the pity. A 240-foot height limit was imposed by the city and the towers improve their immediate vicinity without imposing on the broader skyline.

The towers form the residential component of a mixed-use development consisting mainly of luxury apartments, although 46,000 square feet were set aside for low- and moderate-income housing. There is an office component in this half of the block while the other half is occupied by what used to be a post office.

In fact, the entire project is based around the old Post Office, now listed in the US Register of Historic Places. The building is notable for the strong massing of its Moderne architecture and for the Works Project Administration murals carried out by Anton Refregier in 1940. The shell has been saved but its guts have been scooped out to create a rather overwrought atrium space surrounded by restaurants and offices. A pleasant public walkway cuts across this superblock separating the old Post Office from the towers and creating a small coutyard that is evidently well liked.

ADDRESS 101 Spear Street, SF 94111 [SF/A/CC SF 3 B3]
CLIENT Perini Investment Property, Inc.
STRUCTURAL ENGINEER Chin & Hensolt Engineers
CONTRACT VALUE estimated construction costs $77 million
SIZE 1,000,000 square feet (93,000 square metres)
ACCESS retail components are open

South of Market

Johnson Fain and Pereira Associates 1989

Johnson Fain and Pereira Associates 1989

San Francisco Centre

The San Francisco Centre (note the British spelling) is what is known in the retail trade as a vertical mall. Instead of the horizontal spread of the out-of-town, suburban variety, this urban mall goes up. The strategy of the traditional mall is to position major stores or cinema complexes at either end of rows of smaller shops and let the unsuspecting shopper ping-pong between the major attractions. In the San Francisco Centre the big draw is a Nordstrom store that occupies the top five of the nine floors. Analysts forecast doom for Nordstrom and the Centre partly because of the South of Market location and partly because no-one, they said, would climb two or more floors to get to any store. They were wrong. On the opening day 60,000 people came to the Centre and Nordstrom made sales of $1.5 million. Credit for this must go to Nordstrom's pulling power but also to the architects who have created a reassuring, stolid building that looks as if it could withstand a rocket attack, let alone the modern shopper's greatest foe, the poor.

The façade looks as if it belongs to a bank, with its metal grilles over its (fake) windows. In a thoughtful gesture, it steps back above the fifth floor to avoid casting shadow over the cable car turnaround and Hallidie Plaza across the street. (One of the most intriguing things about this building – apart from its two 60,000-pound-capacity freight elevators that are big enough to hold semitrailer trucks – is the fact that it only casts shadow on the Plaza on 21 March, 21 September and 21 December.)

The main architectural gesture designed to draw the crowds and keep them moving is an oval-shaped atrium that is ringed by 'spiral' escalators and topped by a sliding, glazed roof (chosen not so much for its dramatic effect but primarily because it was quicker and easier to install than a fixed roof.)

The various stores in the mall are unsurprising but they emphasise how

South of Market

Whisler-Patri 1988

Whisler-Patri 1988

thoroughly architecture has been assimilated into the world of retailing. Look, for example, at Adrienne Vittadini's miniaturised Gare d'Orsay. The real interest in the San Francisco Centre, however, is in its potential to act as a model for the rejuvenation of tired city centres.

South of Market

ADDRESS Market Street and 5th Street, SF 94103 [SF/A/CC SF 7 A2]
CLIENT Gordon Company
STRUCTURAL ENGINEER Cygna Consulting Engineers
SIZE 670,000 square feet (62,000 square metres)
ACCESS open

Whisler-Patri 1988

Whisler-Patri 1988

San Francisco Marriott

The Marriott Hotel is variously known as the Wurlitzer, the Jukebox or the CD Player, depending, it seems, on the age of the person you are talking to. That it has any familiar names at all appears to be a sign of its acceptance into the life of the city, although not everyone likes it. According to an unscientific poll, architects don't like it, but other people do.

One thing everybody can agree on is that you notice the Marriott. Located next door to the Yerba Buena Gardens and a short stroll from the Moscone Convention Center, it is far enough from the Financial District to have no real competitors in the high building stakes in its immediate vicinity. You see it from the approach to the Bay Bridge, you see it from Potrero Hill and Twin Peaks, you even see it from the ferry to Tiburon. It is a shame that it has to be so ugly. Everything about it looks cheap and, apparently, is. Evidently the design for the hotel went through many hands and those that left the greatest impression were Marriott's corporate cost-cutters. Particularly unpleasant reflective glass crowns the building in distinctive seashell swirls, 40 feet high and 80 feet across, and porridge-coloured synthetic masonry panels (that look just what they are) clad the rest of the structure.

There is an undeniable glitz to the tower, however, and it is fun to imagine a demented millionaire occupying the shimmering ferris wheels and presiding over an empire of Caligulan debauchery. In fact, the average conventioneer is dispatched to monastic rooms of pygmy proportions and remarkable characterlessness.

Public spaces are relentlessly tacky; Market Street is shamefully ignored; the peculiar ziggurat form of the building is mind-bogglingly asymmetrical; whatever animation the glass arcs provide is negated by the truncated tower; and the viewing galleries – bars, actually – on the 38th floor are a disappointment. The thick black struts that support the

DMJM (Daniel, Mann, Johnson & Mendenhall) 1989

DMJM (Daniel, Mann, Johnson & Mendenhall) 1989

swirls of glass are irredeemably crude and are guaranteed to interfere with your view.

The best view of the hotel is at night from Grant Avenue when darkness shrouds the tower in possibilities. The worst view is from the front of SF MOMA (see page 38) where, after a tour of that building, the shallowness of the Marriott is put into sharp focus.

ADDRESS 55 4th Street, SF 94103 [SF/A/CC SF 7 A2]
CLIENT Marriott Corporation
STRUCTURAL ENGINEER Martin Middlebrook Louie
CONTRACT VALUE $150 million
SIZE 1500 rooms
ACCESS open

DMJM (Daniel, Mann, Johnson & Mendenhall) 1989

DMJM (Daniel, Mann, Johnson & Mendenhall) 1989

Yerba Buena Gardens

Yerba Buena Gardens is an 87-acre area that stretches from Market Street to Harrison Street and east of 3rd Street to west of 4th. A remarkable achievement for the Redevelopment Agency and for the people of San Francisco who were involved in shaping the development process, its history has been turbulent. Spanning approximately forty years, Yerba Buena is coming to fruition despite indecision, acrimony, the bankruptcy of one of its most recent backers (Olympia & York) and the passing of several generations of city governments.

In the 1950s the Yerba Buena district was in decline as heavy industry, shipping trades and associated industries began to leave San Francisco. Yerba Buena was made up largely of light-industrial works and small residential hotels and seemed right for a development that could initiate economic recovery in the neighbourhood and beyond. In 1954 a redevelopment area covering 1100 acres was designated and what was known as the 'Prosperity Plan' was initiated. This soon foundered, however, and it was not until 1964, when a more focused plan – concentrated on the three central blocks bounded by 3rd and 4th and Mission and Folsom Streets – was proposed that impetus was recovered. This plan proposed a model that included a convention centre, theatres, museums, retail outlets and a sports facility. Although it was not implemented, this has remained the basic blueprint for the area.

In 1967 the City's Board of Supervisors approved the Yerba Buena Center Project Redevelopment Plan and Kenzo Tange began to prepare a plan for a 13-million-square-foot mega-structure. By the time the plan was presented in 1969, the ground had been cleared but the scheme was shelved after a class-action suit by local activists was filed on behalf of the dispossessed residents. In 1976 then-mayor George Moscone appointed a select committee to supervise public hearings to determine

1954–

1954–

the character of Yerba Buena. The result of those hearings was the basis for the present plan with a subterranean convention centre and an emphasis on open space, local arts and a mix of housing and business interests. The one major casualty from earlier plans was a sports facility.

In 1981 Moscone South was completed and yet another master plan was drawn up (this time by landscape architects Lawrence Halprin and Omi Lang and architects Ziedler Roberts), inspired by Copenhagen's Tivoli Gardens.

In 1985, after an international search, commissions were awarded to Fumihiko Maki and James Stewart Polshek for the Center for the Arts buildings and to Romaldo Giurgula for the Esplanade Gardens. In 1988 Mario Botta was appointed architect for the new San Francisco Museum of Modern Art after it was decided to relocate the institution in Yerba Buena.

Future developments include towers by James Ingo Freed, of Pei Cobb Freed, and by Cesar Pelli. The Mexican Museum plans to move into the area, as does the California Historical Society. An entertainment complex that will complete the Esplanade Gardens block is due to start construction soon and there are plans to use the roof of Moscone South to house a number of facilities for children as well as a bowling alley and an ice rink.

South of Market

ADDRESS bordered by Market Street and Harrison Street, 3rd Street and 4th Street, SF 94103 [SF/A/CC SF 7 A2–B2]
CLIENT San Francisco Redevelopment Agency
ACCESS open

1954–

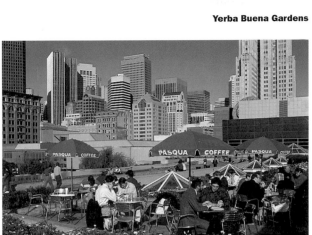

1954–

Esplanade Gardens

The Esplanade Gardens, together with the Center for the Arts, occupy the roofscape of Moscone North. The Moscone Convention Center is the workhorse of Yerba Buena Gardens but the best things that can be said about Moscone North and South is that they are each considerable feats of engineering and that they are both underground. The heroic entrance to Moscone South and the somewhat more tempered and understated North entrance do not suggest that, had the structures been allowed to rise above ground, they would have been anything more than misplaced airport terminals which would have annihilated two full city blocks and any hope of life for blocks around.

The mere existence of the Esplanade and the Arts Center, however, is a humanistic and generous statement that more than makes up for whatever drawbacks Moscone may have. The Gardens were designed as a green space in the city: a place where people can watch outdoor performances, sitting on the grassy banks, or walk the meandering perimeter paths between redwoods, stone pine, maple, plum, weeping willows and liquidambar trees, and even through a butterfly garden. The grassed area is an oval bowl that was formed by creating contours out of great blocks of styrofoam, used to limit the weight on Moscone's roof.

The Center for Visual Arts building borders the Gardens to the north-east, a waterfall and terraced paths that disguise the back of Moscone North's entrance create a backdrop to the south-east, a planned entertainment center by SMWM will enclose the south-west side, while the Gardens open out on to Mission Street, managing to incorporate two emergency exits from the subterranean Moscone, to the north-west. The lawns are overlooked by a pair of cafés, linked by a covered walkway, that sit on top of Moscone North's entrance, together with a pool that flows into the waterfall. Sculpture by a number of artists has been incor-

MGA Partners with Romaldo Giurgola 1993

MGA Partners with Romaldo Giurgola 1993

porated into the plan, as has a memorial to Martin Luther King.

It seems mean-spirited to carp, but the Esplanade lacks something and that is the clear-minded intention to draw together the disparate elements of Yerba Buena. The Gardens' relationship to Maki's serene ocean liner is particularly insensitive and their inability to give this building the room that it deserves is largely responsible for its failure to assert its presence.

However, the only real test for any garden is time and mature trees and established planting may make this area such a beautiful oasis in the city that the buildings will become irrelevant. The design was arrived at through extensive public discussion and so, evidently, the City has what the people wanted, and how much better to have a flawed garden than a perfect mega-structure – even one by Tange.

ADDRESS Yerba Buena Gardens at Mission Street, between 3rd and 4th Streets, SF 94103 [SF/A/CC SF 7 B2]
CLIENT SF Redevelopment Agency with Center for the Arts
STRUCTURAL ENGINEER Rutherford & Chekene
CONTRACT VALUE $40 million
SIZE 5.5 acres (2 hectares)
ACCESS open

South of Market

MGA Partners with Romaldo Giurgola 1993

MGA Partners with Romaldo Giurgola 1993

Yerba Buena Center: Galleries and Forum

Originally, the Center for the Arts commission was intended to be given to one architect but the powers-that-be liked the work of Fumihiko Maki and James Stewart Polshek equally and so decided to split the programme and the commission.

The gallery was not to be a conventional museum and would have no collection of its own but would be a space available to the many arts organisations in San Francisco. It would not be the sort of club for the wealthy that SF MOMA is perceived to be, and it would reflect the ethnic and social diversity of the city. The emphasis would be on visual arts but galleries had to be able to accommodate video, film, theatre and dance as well as painting and sculpture – and even this broad programme was a distillation of initial wish lists derived from public hearings.

There are three galleries of different sizes, a Media Center for film and video, and 'The Forum', a multi-purpose space for theatre, dance, lectures, etc. The interiors are lustrous spaces that connect in unexpected ways and keep one moving easily through the structure.

A courtyard garden best exemplifies Maki's approach to space making. The garden contains a stand of bamboo, rocks and a reflecting pool. Views into the small courtyard are only partially revealed, however, and the impression one is left with is of something distant, mysterious and hard to define.

These characteristics of mystery and revelation are present throughout the interior of the building and also manifest themselves in the exterior. The description of the structure as an 'elegant warehouse' does not come close to doing it justice. Even though corrugated aluminium siding is used extensively, the building has a lightness and delicacy that could never be described as industrial. It might have been more successful if it had

South of Market

Fumihiko Maki & Associates 1993

South of Market

Fumihiko Maki & Associates 1993

embraced a tougher aesthetic. The weakest elevation is the one fronting 3rd Street which makes a half-hearted attempt to relate to the street but ultimately fails. Other elevations are so light they seem to shimmer like a heat haze.

One leaves the building with fragmentary memories: of three curved skylights that set the building in motion, as if they were the three smoke stacks of a liner seen on the distant horizon; of the glass and aluminium wall that faces the Esplanade Gardens, so thin it dissolves the boundary between outside and in; of the boxy superstructure of mechanical functions on the roof that is topped by a tall mast. It is a shame that this building is not given the space it needs to be fully appreciated, but it is its own fault that it does not assert itself on 3rd Street.

South of Market

ADDRESS 701 Mission Street, SF 94103 [SF/A/CC SF 7 B2]
ASSOCIATE ARCHITECTS Robinson Mills+Williams
CLIENT SF Redevelopment Agency with Center for the Arts
STRUCTURAL ENGINEER Structural Design Engineers
CONTRACT VALUE $40 million (with theatre)
SIZE 55,000 square feet (5100 square metres)
ACCESS open

Fumihiko Maki & Associates 1993

Fumihiko Maki & Associates 1993

Yerba Buena Center Theatre

Squeezed into a difficult corner site by the neighbouring Moscone Center, and with the instruction that the primary orientation of the building should be toward the central Esplanade Gardens, Polshek has treated the Center for the Arts Theatre as a piece of sculpture. Each element of the building has been identified, abstracted and then expressed. The fly tower is an angled box clad in a grid of aluminium panels. The auditorium is a cube clad in a grid of bluey-black ceramic tiles, and the proscenium manifests itself as a sliver of aluminium between the two. Foyers are boxes of glass that back on to walls of bright primary colours, and internal circulation areas are revealed by walls of gridded glass. The building is flamboyant and extroverted and just what was called for. It also manages to do what might have seemed impossible – to orient itself (at least to some degree) to all the surrounding streets and buildings. Given that the service entrances had to go somewhere, the theatre even makes a passable appearance on 3rd Street.

The exuberant colours used in the foyers hardly prepare one for the dark and skeletal design of the auditorium, but its eerie and intimate ambiance proves to be an energising force and creates successful theatre in its own right.

ADDRESS Yerba Buena Center for Arts, corner of 3rd and Howard Streets, SF 94103 [SF/A/CC SF 7 B2]
CLIENT SF Redevelopment Agency with Center for the Arts
STRUCTURAL ENGINEER Rutherford & Chekene
CONTRACT VALUE $40 million (with Visual Arts Building)
SIZE 46,000 square feet (4300 square metres), 755 seats
ACCESS open; call for information

James Stewart Polshek & Partners 1993

South of Market

South of Market

James Stewart Polshek & Partners 1993

San Francisco Museum of Modern Art

SF MOMA, opened in January 1995, is Mario Botta's first project built in the United States and his first museum. Botta's pedigree includes time spent studying under Carlo Scarpa, working with Le Corbusier while still a student, and with Louis Kahn shortly after graduating. The monumental abstraction of some of Corbusier's and Kahn's work finds its way into this project but in a form that Botta has made recognisably his own.

Botta's fascination with the circle and the square continues to be explored in this project, while his very personal style is expressed in the meticulously crafted and textured brickwork that forms the stepped boxes of the Museum, and which derive from the architect's Ticinese regionalist sensibilities, and in the striations of light and dark stone on the central atrium which have become almost a trademark.

The nerve of designing a building that emanates from the Swiss cantons but in reality is entirely placeless and then beaming it into houseproud San Francisco is decidedly Modernist in its arrogance. What is even more amazing is that it works. Whatever eternal verities pure geometric form encapsulates, Botta has managed to tap into them. Vaguely evocative of Boullée's tribute to Sir Isaac Newton, SF MOMA is engagingly nutty, although it also has more than a touch of the totalitarian mausoleum about it. Because of this latent grandiosity it is serendipitous that Yerba Buena Arts Center has turned 3rd Street into something of a back alley. Far better to come across this building unexpectedly, glimpsed at an awkward angle across lanes of busy traffic, than to find it deferentially revealed.

SF MOMA's pugnacious stoutness and its lack of deference to the traditions of San Francisco soon become virtues and you know very well that if the two skyscrapers that are proposed to flank the Museum are ever built it will more than hold its own.

South of Market

Mario Botta with Hellmuth Obata & Kassabaum 1994

Mario Botta with Hellmuth Obata & Kassabaum 1994

The plan is based on galleries grouped around the central open space and relates back to the Palladianism of Botta's early houses in Ticino. The atrium is truly grand, although slightly schizophrenic. At ground level it is finished in polished and flamed bands of black granite that create the feel of Islamic architecture, more like a mosque than the cathedral it has been compared to, albeit with a certain Lego-like quality. At its highest point the circular void is crossed by a steel bridge that comes straight out of the machine age. Each gesture seems rather self-conscious, but each has undeniable jaw-dropping potential.

The ultimate test of such a building is whether its galleries work and in this SF MOMA is a huge success. The rooms are tall and spacious and filled with natural light thanks to the way the building is stepped back, creating lots of roof space and consequently lots of skylights.

South of Market

ADDRESS 151 3rd Street, SF 94103 [SF/A/CC SF 7 B2]
CLIENT San Francisco Museum of Modern Art
STRUCTURAL ENGINEER Forrell/Elsesser
CONTRACT VALUE $60 million
SIZE 225,000 square feet (21,000 square metres)
ACCESS open

Mario Botta with Hellmuth Obata & Kassabaum 1994

Yerba Buena Gardens Entertainment and Retail Center

What Yerba Buena seems to lack is a sense of cohesion and it is possible that the Entertainment Center will provide this. Unlike other 'cultural centres', Yerba Buena has sensibly decided to include commercial film in its programme and this building will house fifteen cinemas as well as retail stores and restaurants. The structure will stretch the whole block between Mission and Howard and will feature a 270-foot-long public lobby overlooking the gardens. On 4th Street externally mounted screens will have movies projected on to them to lure pedestrians in.

The possibility that this element of Yerba Buena – so much bigger than anything else – will overwhelm the theatre and gallery has to be a real danger, but it has an even greater potential for being a positive force. The additional people it will bring to the area must be a good thing and the theatre, gallery and SF MOMA will surely benefit from this. The design integrates 4th Street into the overall conception of the Gardens, unlike the poorly treated 3rd Street, and it may well help to leven the lumpish lower floors of the Marriott Hotel.

South of Market

ADDRESS Yerba Buena Gardens on 4th Street SF 94103 [SF/A/CC SF 7 B2]
ASSOCIATED ARCHITECT Gary Handel Associates
CLIENT Millennium Partners & WDG Companies
STRUCTURAL ENGINEER DeSimone, Chaplin & Dobryn
CONTRACT VALUE approximately $52 million
SIZE 354,151 square feet (33,000 square metres)
ACCESS open

Simon Martin-Vegue Winkelstein Moris 1996

Simon Martin-Vegue Winkelstein Moris 1996

Restaurant LuLu

Opening a restaurant a couple of blocks away from a convention centre and a 1500-room hotel was always likely to be a good idea, but the owners of LuLu have added good food and interesting architecture to make their venture a considerable success.

The first ingredient was an 8000-square-foot warehouse. The vaulted Douglas fir roof was sandblasted, simplified by the removal of some beams and peeled back in certain areas to open up skylights. The façade was completely re-jigged to create a form of 'Mediterranean Modernism' that makes a passing reference to Ronchamp, with its curving stucco walls and freely placed windows of coloured glass. Details in the 6000-square-foot main dining area are kept simple to allow the theatre of the large space to play out. Walls are coloured plaster and floors are coloured concrete. Nothing distracts from the focal point of the room, a large brick oven. To orientate the room to this point, the architect has borrowed from Michelangelo's Piazza del Campidoglio in Rome. An ellipse is centred within a trapezium-shaped plan. In this case an oval dining area set on the axis of the ovens is flanked on two sides by higher eating and bar areas.

In the same structure and running on either side of LuLu's are a smaller, narrower dining room painted with a streetscape and with a guest appearance by Le Corbusier's Modular man, and a café. The café also adopts a European style – a harder edged, chicer style out of Milan.

ADDRESS 816 Folsom Street, SF 94107 [SF/A/CC SF 7 B3]
CLIENTS Reed Heron & Louise Clement
STRUCTURAL ENGINEER Preece Goudie
CONTRACT VALUE $720,000 construction
SIZE 8000 square feet (740 square metres)
ACCESS open

South of Market

Cass Calder Smith Architecture 1993

Cass Calder Smith Architecture 1993

1028 Howard Street

The South of Market and Tenderloin districts have traditionally been home to the poor and homeless and, in the area around 6th, 7th and 8th Streets, a number of low-rent apartment blocks are being built to replace decaying hotels and hostels. It is possible to see this part of the city as a containment area for the homeless but, even if this is true, it should not detract from the generosity of spirit that these projects individually manifest nor from the high standards of architecture.

1028 Howard Street contains 30 units designed for low-income families. An elegant and spare structure, it creates an appropriate presence on a busy and generally inhospitable street. Mirroring the San Franciscan standard lot size, the façade is broken into five 25-foot-wide modules, each with a bay window, and separated by 10-foot-wide set-backs. Cement board cladding in three different styles is used: applied in horizontal strips and painted to resemble clapboard; in its bare state on the window bays, and in a corrugated form between some of the flush windows. Stucco is used on the generally blank ground floor.

Apartments are spacious and the only obvious area where costs have been cut is the patio garden at the rear of the building.

South of Market

ADDRESS 1028 Howard Street, SF 94103 [SF/A/CC SF 7 A3]
CLIENT Mercy Charities
STRUCTURAL ENGINEER OLMM
CONTRACT VALUE $3.5 million
SIZE 50,000 square feet (4600 square metres)
ACCESS none

Simon Martin-Vegue Winkelstein Moris 1994

Simon Martin-Vegue Winkelstein Moris 1994

One Trinity Center

This mixed-use development is architecturally something of a capricious hybrid. Its 85-foot-high street façade has a vaguely Viennese feel to it – a touch of Adolf Loos, perhaps – while above this a simple curtain wall, expressed as a tight grid, steps back to a peaked bathing hut complete with flag. The light-coloured concrete façade with its diamond marble inserts and verdigris-coloured balconies, and the *fin-de-siècle* Caffe Trinity on the ground floor, make this building an odd neighbour to the bland box next to it and an unlikely addition to this rather tawdry and dilapidated end of Market Street. The slight sense of unreality is not unpleasant, however, and from a distance the building's 'hat' is an interesting addition to the skyline.

South of Market

ADDRESS 1145 Market Street, SF 94103 [SF/A/CC SF D B1]
CLIENT Trinity Properties
STRUCTURAL ENGINEER John Rutigliano
SIZE 145,000 square feet (13,500 square metres)
ACCESS to Caffe Trinity

Backen, Arrigoni & Ross 1989

South of Market

Backen, Arrigoni & Ross 1989

Advent Software

Advent Software is a company that manages stock portfolios for money managers. Their offices are on the fifth and sixth floors of a 1909 building in the South of Market district. The conversion is all concealed light and brooding, meticulously finished materials. The old concrete pillars have been revealed and act as a foil to squares of dark steel on the floors, squares of aluminium on the walls, wavy panels of acoustical metal hanging from the ceiling and, in lighter vein, maple veneer ply desk panels. A recurring motif is the angled panel: ply panels angle out from desks to form low level screens and columns of aluminium squares flare out as they rise.

One of South Park Fabricators' magnificent staircases – in this case with the handrail used as the truss from which the folded aluminium treads and risers are hung – joins the two levels.

South of Market

ADDRESS 301 Brannan Street, SF 94107 [SF/A/ CC SF 7 C3]
CLIENT Advent Software
STRUCTURAL ENGINEER Stephen Tipping
SIZE 23,000 square feet (2100 square metres)
ACCESS none

MacCracken Architects 1992

MacCracken Architects 1992

Jack London Townhouses

Laid out in 1856 by George Gordon, an Englishman who was evidently inspired by London squares, South Park is now ringed by converted warehouses that give this unexpected oasis in the city a SoHo feel. Jack London Townhouses are four residential units over office space. The basic rectangle of the site is visually split in two by an open stairway that provides access to part of the building. Above the ground floor the mass of the structure is expressed as squares and arcs that break through the skin of the orthogonal boxes.

The building was designed to use non-toxic materials from sustainable sources. The structural elements are lightweight steel which eliminates the need for plywood and other composite wood materials. Recycled newspaper is used for wall and ceiling insulation instead of fibreglass. Wood flooring comes from sustainably managed forests.

When one is told that the building is clad in cement board, copper sheet, ceramic tile, slate and asphalt and copper shingles, you imagine the worst. Rather than being the visual cacophony that this suggests, however, the building's exterior appears considered, measured and entirely appropriate for its setting.

ADDRESS 86 South Park, SF 94107 [SF/A/CC SF 7 B3]
CLIENT Jack London South Park Inc.
STRUCTURAL ENGINEER John Quan
CONTRACT VALUE $1.4 million
SIZE 12,000 square feet (1100 square metres)
ACCESS none

Levy Design Partners 1995

Levy Design Partners 1995

25 Zoe Street

Absolutely lucid in conception and execution, this live/work building on a street of old warehouses is a good example of how simplicity in design and choice of material can create generous spaces at low cost. On a plot of land only 20 feet wide and 75 feet long, the only way to go was up. In the front elevation the mass is expressed as two towers, one containing the usable spaces, the other, smaller, one containing the stairs. A garage and office occupy the ground floor of the larger form with an apartment on the second level and a photographic studio on the top floor. An exposed steel framework braces against earthquakes and gives the street elevation a structural lightness that is emphasised by the glazing, used exclusively to in-fill the second and third floors. The adjacent tower is clad in metal sheet with a recessed portion between the two blocks.

The photographic studio has 20-foot ceilings and is fully glazed front and back but also has skylights and slender side windows. A loft or mezzanine element increases the square footage. Plywood floors, white stucco walls and exposed roof beams are the key elements in the design. The apartment uses a similar vocabulary and is notable for its washes of natural light, its spacious proportions and the clever detailing that allows the minimalist aesthetic to succeed so well. Doors of perspex over wooden frames and a particularly spare kitchen of steel counters and ply cabinets are noteworthy.

ADDRESS 25 Zoe Street, SF 94107 [SF/A/CC SF 7 B3]
CLIENTS Thomas Heinser and Madeleine Corson
STRUCTURAL ENGINEER Tennebaum-Manheim
CONTRACT VALUE construction $365,000
SIZE 4000 square feet (370 square metres)
ACCESS none

South of Market

Tanner Leddy Maytum Stacy 1992

Knox SRO

Knox SRO is built on the site of the Anglo Hotel which fell down in the Loma Prieta earthquake. It is named after Walter Knox, one of the displaced residents of the old rooming house, who had become famous for 'claiming' a piece of waste ground on Clementina Street as a garden for the local people.

Located on the 6th Street Redevelopment corridor, Knox is a single-room-occupancy development designed for very low-income tenants, some of whom will have previously been homeless. There are 140 units in the building (a density equivalent to the mind-boggling figure of 765 units an acre), but this is not apparent from the exterior because each bay window, which one would expect to belong to a single unit, is split down the middle and is in fact shared by two units. Extensive discussions with tenants of other local SROs led the architects to certain design criteria. Noteworthy requests were for high levels of security and surveillance (which in this case includes bulletproof glass) and a preference for shared bathrooms rather than kitchens. There is a roof garden which includes a viewing balcony located between the horns of the split tower (a passing reference to Antonio Sant' Elia) and a small courtyard garden within the L of the footprint.

Concrete sheer walls provide earthquake resistance while the façades are a lightweight skin of coated styrofoam.

ADDRESS 241 6th Street, SF 94103 [SF/A/CC SF D C1]
CLIENT Tenants & Owners Development Corporation
STRUCTURAL ENGINEER Olmm Structural Design
CONTRACT VALUE $8.1 million
SIZE 54,000 square feet (5000 square metres)
ACCESS none

South of Market

Herman Stoller Coliver 1994

Herman Stoller Coliver 1994

Canon Kip

Canon Kip House replaces a building of the same name that provided services to the homeless for nearly 100 years. The Episcopal Community Services of San Francisco, which runs Canon Kip and a number of other facilities in the city, demolished the old building and KMD designed the new structure better to meet the needs of its very low-income residents. There are 105 rooms, providing permanent accommodation for previously homeless men and women. Skills training is an important part of Canon Kip's role and reading, writing and mathematics are taught, as well as money-management skills. The building also serves as a 'Senior Center' for the neighbourhood and a large commercial kitchen to feed visitors is included in the plan.

Rooms are a minimum of 145 square feet and each has its own sink and small refrigerator. Some have separate bathrooms; other, paired, rooms share a bathroom. Residents all have access to a communal kitchen.

The building is distinguished by its corner tower, tiled base, square bays and the way traditional features have been interpreted with a somewhat mannered touch.

South of Market

ADDRESS corner of 8th and Natoma Streets, SF 94103 [SF/A/CC SF D B1]
CLIENT Episcopal Community Services of San Francisco
STRUCTURAL ENGINEER SDE
CONTRACT VALUE $4.9 million construction
SIZE 50,000 square feet (4600 square metres)
ACCESS none

Kaplan McLaughlin Diaz 1993

Kaplan McLaughlin Diaz 1993

271 Shipley Street

It is possible to see the influence of Donald MacDonald, David Sternberg's one-time employer, in these houses on Shipley Street. Like MacDonald, Sternberg has acted as developer of his own project and has transformed a small, out-of-the-way site with attention-seeking architecture. Six houses are compressed on to the site, arranged around a T-shaped entry court. Two of the houses face the mid-block Shipley Street, while the other four look out toward the 80 Freeway, a couple of blocks away. Walls are of brightly coloured plywood with a diamond pattern of diagonal battening. Square bays with stepped parapets are clad in corrugated metal. The major cost- and space-saving factor is the parking which is all at grade and uncovered.

ADDRESS 271 Shipley Street, SF 94107
[SF/A/CC SF D C I]
CLIENT David Sternberg
STRUCTURAL ENGINEER Santos & Urrutia
CONTRACT VALUE $520,000
SIZE six units, 725 to 825 square feet
(67 to 77 square metres)
ACCESS none

Sternberg Architects 1992

Sternberg Architects 1992

7 Hallam Street

The massive earthquake bracing of this condominium building is given prominence in its façade in a bravura gesture. The great steel A is revealed behind a broad window that rises almost the full height of the structure, displaying both the bracing and the flights of stairs that criss-cross in front of the elevator tower. It turns the building into a giant television screen or human ant hill. A saw-toothed roof and galvanised corrugated metal cladding suggest that this could be a refurbished industrial building but it is actually new construction.

ADDRESS 7 Hallam Street, SF 94103 [SF/A/CC SF 7 A3]
CLIENTS Tom Robertson and Jody Jahn
STRUCTURAL ENGINEER Larry Fowler
CONTRACT VALUE $1.1 million
SIZE 11,000 square feet (1000 square metres)
ACCESS none

South of Market

Seigal & Strain Architects 1992

Seigal & Strain Architects 1992

Hallam Street Houses

These houses might have been designed by Dr Who, with their armadillo scales of glass over bay windows, perky skylights and metal cladding. Each no more than 12 feet wide, but very deep, the houses need to pull in as much light as they can and the idiosyncratic fronts are designed to facilitate this. Dormer windows located amidships, where the structures step up from two to three levels, further assist.

Internal spaces are designed to be as flexible as possible, particularly on the ground floor where the garage and adjoining study/utility room offer the greatest potential for change.

Next door to this pair of houses is a row of buildings by the same architect that also capitalise on tall internal spaces and are similarly idiosyncratic in their expression.

South of Market

ADDRESS 33 and 35 Hallam Street, SF 94103 [SF/A/CC SF 7 A3]
CLIENT Donald MacDonald
STRUCTURAL ENGINEER Uno Veideman
SIZE 1200 square feet (110 square metres) each unit
ACCESS none

MacDonald Architects 1990

MacDonald Architects 1990

The Design Office of Wong & Yeo

This old machine shop was gutted, the roof pulled off and the façade removed to convert it into a large, high, open, tranquil space.

The new façade is a grid of exposed steel moment framing that is infilled with sheet-steel and glass elements. The industrial sash windows and the large garage door give emphasis to the central section of the grid.

The simple structural elements are reflected indoors by a large open space that rises the full height of the building. Mezzanines at the front and rear of the space increase usable square footage and are linked by a bridge that runs along one wall and is suspended from the new ceiling trusses by slender steel rods. Three-quarter-inch sheets of sanded plexi-glass are used for the deck of the bridge, giving it an ethereal lightness. If the exterior is a little too square, a little too rigid, the interior is magical.

South of Market

ADDRESS 146 11th Street, SF 94103 [SF/A/CC SF D B2]
CLIENTS Valerie Wong and Hock Yeo
STRUCTURAL ENGINEER Tennebaum-Manheim
CONTRACT VALUE $185,000 construction cost
SIZE 3500 square feet (325 square metres)
ACCESS none

Tanner Leddy Maytum Stacy 1993

1022 Natoma Street

If anything, this project is too close to perfection. This live/work building housing the architect's offices is located on a narrow street in one of the grittier parts of the South of Market area and, despite a contextual rhetoric, is undoubtedly an intruder. An exposed steel moment frame defines the front elevation and creates an armature from which the various floors seem to hang. They protrude to form a central bay, flanked by staircases, but the horizontal window strips immediately distance it from its neighbours.

This is a quiet and enjoyably dingy street and one cannot help feeling that the building is just too well finished for its tatty neighbours. It would feel more at home on an out-of-town industrial park or next to the runway of a major airport. It lacks the ugly beauty of the nearby warehouses.

The backside of 1022, however, is a different matter: it is much uglier and much more likeable. A wall of cement board angles out from the building, ostensibly to catch as much natural light as possible, and its bluntness is a tonic.

South of Market

ADDRESS 1022 Natoma Street, SF 94103 [SF/A/CC SF D B2]
CLIENT Natoma Group
SIZE 7000 square feet (650 square metres)
ACCESS none

Stanley Saitowitz 1992

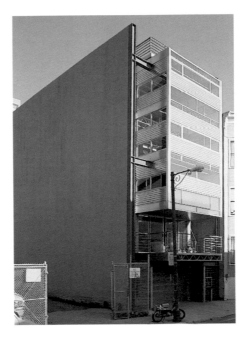

Stanley Saitowitz 1992

940 Natoma Street Lofts

In comparison to some of the nearby houses, this project might be considered tame. Its form is conventional and its use of materials – even the over-used metal siding that is usually considered the password to hipness – is restrained. Nevertheless, it is this quality of restraint that makes it a success.

The double-fronted façade is split in two by a strip of corrugated steel and the two bays are also metal-clad. Unpainted plaster work dominates elsewhere. Curved pediments crown the bays with circular vents used as decorative elements.

ADDRESS 940 Natoma Street, SF 94L03 [SF/A/CC SF D B2]
CLIENT Natoma Street Associates
STRUCTURAL ENGINEER Santos & Urrutia
SIZE 12,000 square feet (1100 square metres)
ACCESS none

Mitchell Benjamin 1994

South of Market

Mitchell Benjamin 1994

SOMA Office

This project converts an old warehouse into a workshop and set of offices for a construction company. Within the office portion, a large two-storey volume has been inserted, dividing the warehouse unequally. An outward sloping wall faced in ply defines the volume on one side while white-painted walls take on a more modular appearance on the other. The ply wall has the massiveness of a ship and sits in the shell of the bowstring truss warehouse like an ark. Its skin of ply is cut into by brightly painted tunnels that penetrate the mass and by a thin slit of windows, placed high on the structure.

If this inscrutable plane, which seems to deny a human factor in its existence, is vaguely unsettling, its obverse is equally so. On this side human existence is readily acknowledged but only as a part of the machine. On this side everything is painted a clinical white. The intruding structure has pushed insubstantial office cubicles up against the warehouse's wall, its bulk and a cantilevered catwalk pinning them there. Spars from the catwalk reach out to link it forcibly with the existing shell, and from below it looks as if the new spars and struts have mingled with the trusses of the vaulted ceiling. The new structure has a beautiful but malign presence, one side showing the grace of its form, the other the relentlessness of its mechanism.

ADDRESS 333 12th Street, SF 94103 [SF/A/CC SF D B2]
CLIENT Ryan Associates
STRUCTURAL ENGINEER Ray Lindahl
CONTRACT VALUE $450,000
SIZE 8140 square feet (760 square metres)
ACCESS none

South of Market

Holt Hinshaw Pfau Jones 1991

South of Market to Mission Bay

Bayside Village

Bayside Village is part of the San Francisco Redevelopment Agency's plan to rejuvenate the old dockside area of South Beach and was designed to create 'affordable rental housing'. It has certainly succeeded. The 8.6-acre site contains 855 apartments (nearly an incredible 100 units per acre) in eight four-storey blocks and one six-storey tower. Rents range from approximately $800 to $1500 for apartments ranging from 475 to 1050 square feet. Amenities include three swimming pools and a health club. Despite the high densities, the architects have attempted to deny the size of the various blocks by inserting tree-lined streets and landscaped gardens into the large site and maintaining a relatively small scale.

The overriding impression this 'urban village' gives, however, is of a bland, inward-looking mega-development that adds almost nothing to the greater community. Lacking the spirit of either Steamboat Point or Delancey Street, Bayside Village highlights the weaknesses of block-by-block development. Steamboat Point and Delancey Street succeed because of their light-hearted architecture but also because of their relatively compact size. The Redevelopment Agency cannot hand over large tracts of land to developers and expect richly urbanistic schemes. A token pedestrian street in a development that explicitly repudiates its connection to the neighbourhood – with its go-nowhere streets and security-gated enclosures – does not make an environment that enriches the city.

ADDRESS 1st Street and Brannan, SF 94107 [SF/A/CC/ SF 7 2C]
CLIENTS Forest City Development and General Atlantic Development
STRUCTURAL ENGINEER GFDF
CONTRACT VALUE $60 million
SIZE 1.1 million square feet (102,000 square metres)
ACCESS limited

Fisher-Friedman Associates 1988/89/90

Fisher-Friedman Associates 1988/89/90

Delancey Street Foundation

Even more interesting than the architecture of this project is the story behind it. The Delancey Street Foundation is a rehabilitation programme for drug users, former convicts, unemployable welfare recipients and the homeless that aims to prepare its residents for a life of useful work. Founded in San Francisco in 1971, the Foundation now has five locations around the country. Unpaid vocational training in businesses run by the Foundation is the cornerstone of the programme and during the minimum two-year stay each resident receives a high-school-equivalent education and is trained in at least three marketable skills. No professional staff are employed and the Foundation accepts no government funding. Self-reliance and co-operation are stressed and the Foundation's various businesses – a moving company, a print works, a restaurant and others – help to finance the operation.

In this spirit, the residents of Delancey Street constructed these buildings themselves. Working with Apersey Construction as general contractor and assisted by the San Francisco Trades Council, 250 residents (about 80 per cent of the workforce) contributed. Many have subsequently found work in construction. Many individuals and companies donated materials and professional services, helping to keep construction costs down to $14 million, approximately half the amount quoted by contractors when the plans were put out to bid. $6 million of this was loaned by the Bank of America in a custom-designed, unsecured line of credit (and paid back ahead of schedule) while the rest came from the foundation's own resources except for $1 million of one-time grants.

No commercial developer had expressed an interest in building the low-income housing that the city's Redevelopment Agency stipulated for the site. This provided Delancey Street with the opportunity to centralise their operation in one complex. Backen, Arrigoni & Ross were engaged

Backen, Arrigoni & Ross 1990

as architects and began a seven-year process – four years paid pro bono – that resulted in these rather unlikely rows of fake Italian tenements that are actually 177 units of communal housing around a courtyard. Residents were involved in the design process and all evinced a preference for more traditional styles of architecture. Modern work apparently evoked unhappy associations with correctional facilities. Evidently it was not a bad choice as the market rate for individual units, if converted to condominiums, would be in the region of $350,000.

The popularity of the architecture is easy to understand: it has a richness and attention to detail that modern architecture often lacks. Although the three blocks that line the triangular site are only dressed boxes, they are well dressed. Verticality is stressed and a rhythmic two-window-wide unit is established by recessed portions and by colour changes. Curved balconies make irregular appearances along the façades and the quality of detailing is extraordinarily high. Clay roof tiles, carved eaves brackets, recessed casement windows, each with a planted window box, and copper downpipes provide visual interest.

Fortuitously, the Embarcadero has been newly planted with palm trees and the illusion that you could be in Cannes or Algiers is easily conjured. When the street-level retail units are all in operation this building will make an even greater contribution to the changing neighbourhood.

ADDRESS 600 Embarcadero, SF 94107 [SF/A/CC SF 7 C2]
CLIENT Delancey Street Foundation
STRUCTURAL ENGINEER Robinson Meier Juilly
CONTRACT VALUE $31 million
SIZE 336,700 square feet (31,300 square metres)
ACCESS restaurant and some retail open

Backen, Arrigoni & Ross 1990

South of Market to Mission Bay

Steamboat Point

Developed under the auspices of the San Francisco Redevelopment Agency by a non-profit housing corporation, this project aims to provide accommodation for low- and very-low-income families. Designed by the same architects as the Delancey Street Foundation (see page 78), it adopts a similarly anti-modern stance but does not suffer because of that.

Once again the strength of the design is in the massing. In this case the rhythms are less obvious, but verticality is again stressed. The clusters of bays at varying heights together with the range of window sizes create a vernacular touch that belies the bulk of the project and its modest budget. The minimally decorated and slightly oversized eaves that extend around all elevations create an odd Etruscan profile that makes you look at traditional San Franciscan Victorian eaves in a completely new light.

A rather austere courtyard, which one imagines must be too small to provide adequate play space for the children, sits in the middle of the lot but a daycare facility has also been provided. Each of the triangular site's three sides has been planted and this helps considerably in linking the buildings to the neighbourhood and makes up for the lack of a street orientation.

ADDRESS Embarcadero/Townsend/King Streets, SF 94107
[SF/A/CC SF 7 C3]
CLIENT Bridge Housing
STRUCTURAL ENGINEER Robinson Meier Juilly
CONTRACT VALUE $65 per square foot
SIZE 115,000 square feet (10,700 square metres)
ACCESS none

South of Market to Mission Bay

Backen, Arrigoni & Ross 1992

South of Market to Mission Bay

Backen, Arrigoni & Ross 1992

The South Embarcadero

Although not strictly speaking a work of architecture, the recently completed stretch of the Embarcadero that replaces the old twin-deck freeway in the South Beach neighbourhood is one of the most successful acts of place-making in San Francisco.

The Embarcadero Freeway was badly damaged in the 1989 Loma Prieta earthquake and was demolished soon after. This has opened up the waterfront so wonderfully that it is hard to imagine how the Freeway was ever allowed to be built in the first place. (It should be noted that in 1982 the City studied a number of alternatives to the Embarcadero Freeway and recommended demolition. The citizens of San Francisco voted not to tear the structure down.)

With the Freeway gone there is now a waterfront promenade that ranges between 25 and 40 feet wide. An element of this is what is projected to be the 'longest permanent artwork in the nation', a 2.5-mile-long strip of concrete which varies in height along its length so it can be used as a bench or a table or simply as a wall and which has a strip of glass block embedded in it which is illuminated by fibre optics (by Vito Acconci, Barbara Stauffacher Solomon and Stanley Saitowitz).

The real success of the Embarcadero, however, is the way it fulfils its fuction with restraint. The DPW team did not want to distract from the waterfront, and design and execution are examples of a rich thoughfulness that is modest without being anonymous, textured and crafted without being showy. Twin roadways flank a pair of light-rail tracks which are separated from the roads by median strips of what looks like Belgian cobblestone but are in fact especially fabricated and much cheaper concrete lookalikes. The tracks are set in a dark concrete studded with pebbles of La Paz stone. These materials are designed to create maintainence-free surfaces that discourage skateboarders, cyclists and pedes-

City and County of San Francisco Department of Public Works 1994

City and County of San Francisco Department of Public Works 1994

tians from attempting to use the potentially dangerous zones. Slightly hokey acorn street lights line the medians but they are far from offensive and tend to disappear beside the one truly theatrical gesture: an avenue of 65 Canary Island palms. Their appropriateness was the subject of a heated debate but they eventually won out on the basis of various performance specifications and a poll conducted via radio, newspapers and community meetings. They are a little unlikely, but one only has to walk down Dolores Street to see that they will not be the first palms to line a street in San Francisco, and their raffishness is hard not to like.

ADDRESS The Embarcadero from King Street/3rd Street north, SF 94107 [SF/A/CC SF 7 C3]
CLIENT Port of San Francisco
ENGINEERS DPW
CONTRACT VALUE $62 million
LENGTH 1 mile (approximately 1.6 kilometres); to be extended
ACCESS open

City and County of San Francisco Department of Public Works 1994

City and County of San Francisco Department of Public Works 1994

Mission Bay Golf Center

Since San Francisco is a city of many cultures, it should not surprise anyone to know that a building type more common in Japan than in the US exists, hidden in the post-industrial landscape of Mission Bay: the golf driving range. Designed by Studios, an architectural firm better known for its work for large, hi-tech companies in Silicon Valley, the range is pleasingly incongruous, close to a dull canal lined with ramshackle house-boats and between anonymous warehouses.

The driving range is 285 yards long on a 9.25-acre site that includes a putting green and café. The tees are positioned along a double-decked platform that has a roof of curved corrugated steel that gently arcs the width of the site. Exposed I-beams provide the structural framework, with the second tier cantilevered over the first.

ADDRESS 1200 6th Street at Channel Street, SF 94107 [SF/A/CC SF 11 B1]
CLIENT Mission Bay Golf Center
STRUCTURAL ENGINEER Robinson Meier Juilly
ACCESS open

Studios 1992

Studios 1992

North of Market /
North Beach

388 Market Street

The collision of two different street grids at Market Street creates a number of triangular sites where Market cuts its diagonal path. No. 388 occupies the smallest of these sites and SOM's tower confidently updates the tradition of flatiron buildings.

The first two floors are given over to retail spaces and they follow the triangular site lines. Above these, the builing adopts a more sculpted teardrop form as a cylindrical tower finds expression within the triangle. A mechanical floor, distinguished by slit windows, and a high cornice tie the cylinder into the triangle both visually and structurally. The mechanical floor divides the sixteen flush-glazed office floors from the residential floors, highlighted by recessed French doors.

The clear expression of functional and geometric components and the use of a polished red granite make this one of San Francisco's very few notable towers. The unusual site has obviously been instrumental in this and points to the importance of limiting the bulk of buildings as well as – indeed, maybe more than – the height.

ADDRESS 388 Market Street, SF 94111 [SF/A/CC SF E C3]
CLIENT Honorway Investment Corporation
STRUCTURAL ENGINEER SOM
CONTRACT VALUE $52 million
SIZE 374,000 square feet (34,700 square metres)
ACCESS limited

North of Market / North Beach

Skidmore Owings & Merrill 1986

Skidmore Owings & Merrill 1986

345 California Center

Like SOM's 388 Market (see page 92), 345 California is distinguished by an unusual site plan treated in a way that attempts to utilise what could be a hindrance and to exploit the potential for unexpected form. The building actually rises in the centre of a block with four older and historically significant buildings anchoring the corners. The 47 above-grade storeys rise 600 feet and are made up of layers of retail and office space until the tower bifurcates into two eleven-storey towers of hotel rooms, linked by glazed skybridges.

ADDRESS 345 California Street, SF 94111 [SF/A/CC SF E C2]
CLIENT Norland Properties
STRUCTURAL ENGINEER SOM
CONTRACT VALUE $83 million
SIZE 880,000 square feet (82,000 square metres)
ACCESS limited

Skidmore Owings & Merrill 1985

North of Market / North Beach

Skidmore Owings & Merrill 1985

Cypress Club

Jordan Mozer is a Chicago architect who makes a living designing phantasmagoric restaurants from Germany to Japan. The Cypress Club is his take on San Francisco and, although it could easily be dismissed as an overblown extravagance, such a judgement ignores both the huge element of fun and the unexpected references to a time and a place. The place is, of course, San Francisco; the time, the 1940s.

The name of the Cypress Club is borrowed from a nightclub featured in Raymond Chandler's *The Big Sleep*, and this manifestation simulates at least some of the loucheness of the original. However, the pregnant beams, swollen columns and pendulous lights belong more in the realm of *Disney Visits Dr Freud* than the cynical world of a *noir* thriller.

The restaurant takes some features – a bar in the main eating space, high wainscoting, intimate seating, velvet draperies, leaded glass, dark woods, tile floors and copper and bronze metalwork – from classic San Franciscan eating places and gives them a twist. Paintwork has been given the yellowy patina of years of cigarette smoke and conversation.

The swollen forms are inspired by American industrial design from the 1940s (particularly influential was a 1948 Hudson). In addition to the fat columns and beams, low walls of curved and quilted copper define spaces and surround you in club-like booths. Mozer's mural above the dark wainscoting depicts a tour of northern California, and was inspired by the work of Thomas Hart Benton, a WPA artist.

ADDRESS 500 Jackson Street, SF 94133 [SF/A/CC SF E B2]
CLIENT John Cunin
CONTRACT VALUE $2 million
SIZE 8800 square feet (820 square metres)
ACCESS open

Jordan Mozer & Associates 1990

Jordan Mozer & Associates 1990

340 Lombard Street

This house occupies a large site and is set back from the street, making no attempt to fill the gap between its neighbours. Two wings emerge from a concrete cylinder that is both the circulation spine of the building and the theatrical highlight. Stairs ascend behind an elevator within the tower and two glass and steel bridges span it. It also acts as a lookout tower, with an open viewing deck on its opaque glass roof.

Not surprisingly, every other opportunity to capitalise on the views of the Marina and Golden Gate Bridge is taken and almost every room is extensively glazed.

North of Market / North Beach

ADDRESS 340 Lombard Street, San Francisco 94133
ACCESS none

James Jennings Arkhitekture 1996

James Jennings Arkhitekture 1996

Glickman Residence

The architects have created an impeccable reinterpretation of the bow-fronted row house that also pays homage to the early modernism of architects such as Pierre Chareau in concrete, enamelled aluminium panels and glass-block. A ground-floor garage is flanked by two doors, the poured-in-place concrete walls providing a visually strong base for the three floors above it. A semi-circular bay of glass-block with various sized cutouts for conventional windows is centrally located, with vertical strip windows on either side. Normal proportion is avoided with the first of these three levels having the lowest ceiling height and the second level having the highest. This is not distracting, however, and the elevation is read as a unity with strongly vertical energy.

ADDRESS 210 Francisco Street, SF 94133 [SF/A/ CC SF 3 A2]
CLIENT Rubin Glickman
STRUCTURAL ENGINEER Lee Mason
SIZE 2500 square feet (230 square metres)
ACCESS none

Backen, Arrigoni & Ross 1985

Backen, Arrigoni & Ross 1985

Martin Residence

The slightly enigmatic, anthropomorphic exterior of this warehouse conversion does not immediately identify it as a family residence. Once past the tall front doors, however, one enters a series of spaces that have the sophistication of a penthouse apartment. A broad entrance hall directs one toward the recesses of the structure and a series of layered spaces. The basic skeleton of the building – the trusses that support the barrel-vaulted roof – have been left exposed and the in-fill walls and ceilings hang from them or skirt around them as if the newly created spaces were modules plugged into the carcass of the old warehouse. The living rooms are grouped around a central courtyard that has been cut into the heart of the structure and glazed walls make this the focal point of the interior. Bedrooms are on a second floor, tucked tightly into the curve of the roof and accessed by an open-tread steel stair. Beyond the courtyard the building retains its original scale and a large studio space is created.

ADDRESS 2135 Powell Street, SF 94133 [SF/A/ CC SF E B1]
CLIENTS David and Kathy Martin
STRUCTURAL ENGINEER P Theodore Anderson
SIZE 2300 square feet (210 square metres) living; 1200 square feet (110 square metres) studio
ACCESS none

Tanner Leddy Maytum Stacy 1987

Tanner Leddy Maytum Stacy 1987

Civic Center to Pacific Heights

Tenderloin AIDS Resource Center

This part of the Tenderloin is about as close to hell as San Francisco gets. Homeless people stand in line for food or accommodation at charitable establishments or simply mill around on street corners. Anybody who has ever rationalised not giving money to a beggar should come down to the Tenderloin.

The AIDS Resource Center is a store-front facility offering free counselling, information and testing. The Center works on a very tight budget and the architects were given two stipulations: that design and construction had to be completed as cheaply as possible, and that construction work would be carried out by unskilled local labour as job-training. In another move to keep costs down, the architects worked *pro bono*.

The architects opened up the old storefront space, finding skylights behind a dropped ceiling, and they have revealed the full 18-foot height. The room is 16 feet wide and 100 feet deep and the architects have highlighted these proportions by stepping a row of offices down the length of the room and up to a mezzanine at the rear. Roofs were left off spaces that did not need to be private so they could be lit by the row of track lights that run along a diagonal beam supported above the offices.

Materials were kept as simple as possible and vinyl tile, plastic laminate and oriented strand board predominate.

ADDRESS 187 Golden Gate Avenue, SF 94102 [SF/A/CC SF D B1]
CLIENT Tenderloin AIDS Network
CONTRACT VALUE $63,000
SIZE 2288 square feet (210 square metres)
ACCESS open

Civic Center to Pacific Heights

FACE Architecture 1991

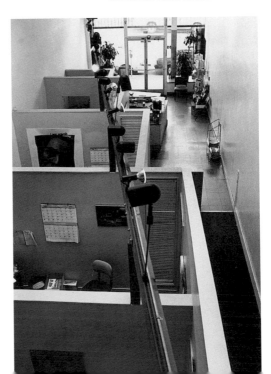

San Francisco Main Library

The Civic Center, described by Sally B Woodbridge as one of the City Beautiful Movement's crowning achievements, is the context for the new Main Library. Given the sensitive site, the architects have settled for reverence. While some lobbyists wanted the new building to mirror the old exactly (in the way that the 1916 building credited to George Kelham is a copy of the Boston Public Library of 1887 by McKim Mead & White, itself inspired by the Bibliothèque Sainte-Geneviève in Paris), the architects have opted to 'reflect and reinterpret' the older structure.

The L-shaped 'honorific front' that looks out on to the Plaza takes its dimensions from the old library but the detail is reworked in a modern idiom. The dangers of this approach are obvious. Where the old library offered deeply recessed windows, a richly decorated entablature and a sense of mass, the new library offers awkward glazing, less than successful decorative features and an obviously thin skin. This might all be forgiven if the ground between the two buildings becomes the magnificent public space that it could be, but the ghastly Civic Center plaza is evidence that San Francisco has a poor record in dealing with its public areas.

The Market Street corner of the new library is unashamedly modern and better for it, but it is the interior that is the real success. A huge circular atrium and a very well handled 'linear atrium' are bravura gestures that work both functionally and aesthetically.

ADDRESS 100 Larkin Street at Fulton, SF 94102 [SF/A/CC SF 6 C3]
ASSOCIATED ARCHITECT Simon Martin-Vegue Winkelstein Moris
STRUCTURAL ENGINEER OLMM
CONTRACT VALUE $87 million construction
SIZE 376,000 square feet (35,000 square metres)
ACCESS open

Pei Cobb Freed & Partners with SMWM 1996

Pei Cobb Freed & Partners with SMWM 1996

Fulton Grove Townhouses

Fulton Grove recapitulates the traditional San Franciscan form of the mid-block lane. Sixteen three-storey townhouses, clad in cedar shingle, line the paved lane with two larger structures at each end. The Fulton Street elevation matches the scale of the neighbouring buildings and its entrance is marked by a bridge spanning the lane. The site narrows to the south and the Grove Street entrance is more tunnel-like, running beneath a tall, more modernistic, clapboard structure.

Features seen in Solomon's Gleeson Residence – gridded windows, strapped chimney flue – are mixed with the arched or bridged entrances seen at Del Carlo Court and Beideman Place. Crennelated roof-lines and alternating patterns of glazing further refine and modernise Solomon's interpretation of the vernacular.

ADDRESS 443 Fulton Street, SF 94102
[SF/A/CC SF 6 B3]
CLIENT Urban Frontier Development
Corporation
STRUCTURAL ENGINEER Peter Culley &
Associates
CONTRACT VALUE $2.3 million construction
SIZE 30,080 square feet (2800 square
metres) gross
ACCESS none

Solomon, Inc. 1992

Rosa Parks Senior Apartments

Before this eleven-storey block was reincarnated as the Rosa Parks Senior Apartments, it was the Yerba Buena Plaza Annex, otherwise known as the 'Pink Palace', an especially unsuccessful housing project built in the early 1960s. Photographs of the Pink Palace show a slab of sleek Modernism, banded by the strong verticals of open balconies. It has a look of confidence and clarity of purpose. It was only when people moved in that things started to go wrong. Balconies were windswept and inhospitable affairs that worked against any form of neighbourliness; entrances allowed anybody – resident or not – to roam the building; ground-floor apartments were particularly susceptible to break-ins and were eventually abandoned; parking lots surrounded the structure. The Pink Palace soon fell into decline and demolition was considered. What the City decided to do instead was to convert the building to housing for the elderly.

Balconies were enclosed to create more hospitable entrances. Although this denies the structure its strong articulation, the boxiness of the new form is alleviated by a very subdued postmodern allusion to classical form. The lowest two floors are painted mustard-yellow, forming a plinth, while an entablature is suggested at the eleventh floor by an architrave painted the same yellow together with a cornice that rings the top of the structure in terracotta. The mass of the building is further broken up by painting areas of the otherwise white walls in shades of cloudy-grey.

The long, and now enclosed, balconies were given some character by the addition of columns and beams that enclose duct-work from the kitchens. Although entirely functional, their symbolic role is even more important in that they help to define – together with window boxes and small benches by the front doors – the space belonging to each apartment.

Working with a Berkeley social scientist, Clare Cooper Marcus, the architects created a number of different communal areas to encourage

Marquis Associates with Young & Associates 1985

Marquis Associates with Young & Associates 1985

social interaction in as many different ways as possible. These spaces range from the overtly social, such as the lounges and the sun room, to the ostensibly functional, such as the mail room and the laundries.

True to the spirit of the civil rights activist for whom the building is named, Rosa Parks has a diverse ethnic mix and signs are posted in four languages. There are no fixed rental rates as such: instead residents pay 30 per cent of their income.

Although this building may not solve housing problems, it does at least suggest ways to deal with buildings that thought they could solve housing problems and it shows how older people can live with dignity.

ADDRESS 1251 Turk Street, SF 94115 [SF/A/CC SF 6 B3]
CLIENT San Francisco Housing Authority
STRUCTURAL ENGINEER Peter Culley & Associates
CONTRACT VALUE $9.2 million
SIZE 29,000 square feet (2700 square metres)
ACCESS none

Marquis Associates with Young & Associates 1985

Marquis Associates with Young & Associates 1985

Oak Street Condos

This condominium development in the Haight district follows a pattern developed by the architect of using distinctive architecture to create small, relatively inexpensive, low-rise dwellings on urban in-fill sites.

The six condos cluster tightly around an inner courtyard that serves as parking for four cars. Only two covered garages are available. Façades employ both sharp angles and curved surfaces and the board and batten cladding is painted in bright primary colours. The development is actually split into two halves of three units each in order to circumvent the City's expensive regulations that come into force if you build four or more condos. The site is of particular interest because it adjoins one of MacDonald's earlier models for creating affordable housing in the city.

ADDRESS 1031–1039 Oak Street, SF 94117 [SF/A/CC SF 10 A1]
CLIENT MacDonald & Nagle
STRUCTURAL ENGINEER Santos & Urrutia
SIZE units at 839, 1212, 1278 square feet (80, 110, 120 square metres)
ACCESS none

MacDonald Architects 1994

MacDonald Architects 1994

Haight Street Lofts

Haight Street Lofts comprise twenty apartments – seventeen market rate, three 'affordable' – built in two blocks separated by a courtyard over the old Luxor Taxicab garage. The architects use their established vocabulary of low-maintenance industrial materials in a very low-key and contextual way. The Haight Street elevation is made up of five bays which emulate the surrounding Victorians but – with their steel panels and exaggerated eaves-brackets – hardly mimic them. The second block is located behind this street-side block and the two are connected by swashbuckling, heavy-timbered bridges that cross the courtyard at two levels. The imagery is heavily industrial, and ironically so since the exposed steel stairways, catwalks and salvaged steel-framed windows that are used as decorative balustrades, create a stage set that is maybe a little too oppressive – too close to the real thing for one to be able to romanticise it successfully. No doubt when the apartments are occupied there will be many human-ising individual touches that will soften the image.

The apartments themselves are double height, some with 16-foot-high walls of glass at the front and rear, with a central core of kitchen and bath-room below and bedroom, study and second bathroom above. The high ceilings and the views from the smaller spaces into the larger make the apartments seem bigger than they are. Five lofts have their own patio gardens while all look out on to the courtyard.

ADDRESS 645 Haight Street, SF 94102 [SF/A/CC SF 10 B1]
CLIENT Haight Street Lofts Inc.
STRUCTURAL ENGINEER Santos & Urrutia
CONTRACT VALUE $1.6 million construction costs
SIZE 20,000 square feet (1900 square metres)
ACCESS none

Tanner Leddy Maytum Stacy 1994

Tanner Leddy Maytum Stacy 1994

The Urban School

The Urban School is a private high school located in the Haight Ashbury district. SMWM drew up a master plan for the reorganisation of the school's existing buildings and have recently completed a structure that houses three classrooms, a computer lab, faculty work areas, a library and parking. The building adopts a residential demeanour, although its razor-sharp detailing and bright yellow stucco make it less modest than this might sound. The central bay offers the architects an opportunity to reinterpret the vernacular in their spare yet detail-oriented style.

Internal spaces are functional and more or less unremarkable until one reaches the library on the third floor. Book stacks are gathered in a central, low-ceilinged core and the confined and darker spaces of this area are used to theatrical effect to contrast the higher, lighter reading rooms at either end of the stacks. The tall and light-filled reading room that overlooks the street is dominated by extensive glazing and a curved ceiling of acoustic metal. A smaller reading room at the rear is treated to a decorative ceiling pattern of arcs that play with perspective.

ADDRESS 1563 Page Street, SF 94117 [SF/A/CC SF 10 A1]
CLIENT The Urban School
STRUCTURAL ENGINEER Dominic Chu
CONTRACT VALUE $2.5 million
SIZE 8500 square feet (800 square metres)
ACCESS none

Simon Martin-Vegue Winkelstein Moris 1994

Civic Center to Pacific Heights

Simon Martin-Vegue Winkelstein Moris 1994

Campus Library, University of California San Francisco

The Campus Library manages to perform the useful function, in an urban design sense, of softening the megalithic structures that dominate the UCSF campus and tower intimidatingly over the Mount Sutro locality. No building could actually domesticate the scale of these behemoths but the library is at least a thoughtful transition. Its own bulk is broken into a number of elements that step back up the hillside in a haphazard ziggurat and, in their very ordinariness, are just what the location called for.

The plainness of the façades does not work so well on Parnassus Avenue, however, where the building reveals itself as rather bland.

Interiors are another matter and here simplicity has been rendered in a rich and inviting way. Attractive woodwork in the form of desks, panelling and other decorative features gives each floor a warmth that such a large institutional building hardly had a right to expect. Reading rooms particularly have the feel of a gentlemen's club. The architects have not made this building completely inward-looking, however, as it would have been foolish to ignore some of the best views in San Francisco, and they exploit these to the maximum.

The library deals with more than 650,000 users anually and its collection is planned to rise to 700,000 volumes.

ADDRESS Parnassus Avenue, SF 94143 [SF/A/CC SF 9 B2]
CLIENT University of California
STRUCTURAL ENGINEER Rutherford & Chekene
CONTRACT VALUE $32 million construction
SIZE 120,000-square-foot (11,000-square-metre) library; 80,000-square-foot (7500-square-metre) underground parking
ACCESS limited

Esherick Homsey Dodge & Davis 1990

Esherick Homsey Dodge & Davis 1990

Park View Commons

Sandwiched between two characterful Art Deco gymnasiums which are the only survivors of the Polytechnic High School demolished in the late 1970s, Park View Commons is a 114-unit affordable housing scheme on a large site in the Haight district between Carl and Frederick Streets.

Three-storey buildings containing flats front the streets while two-storey cottages occupy the mid-blocks. Individual garage parking under the flats lines internal streets and small courtyard gardens and landscaped stairways break up the mass of the buildings. Part San Francisco vernacular, part Italian hill town, the project is largely aesthetically successful although the low budget ($47 a square foot) is apparent in some places.

The real interest in this project, however, lies in its innovative leasing arrangements, unfamiliar in the US. In a long drawn-out process, the City obtained the land from the local school board at a nominal rate on a 75-year lease. The development company – the Bridge Housing Corporation, a noted low-cost housing developer – together with Pacific Union Development Company and the Federal body HUD (Housing and Urban Development Administration) then built the properties which were sold leasehold, rather than freehold, with the city subsidising costs to lower unit prices. To counter speculation the city has a four-year option on the properties and a permanent right of first refusal to purchase any units that are offered for sale.

ADDRESS Frederick Street at Kezar Stadium, SF 94117 [SF/A/CC SF 9 C2]
CLIENT Bridge Housing Corporation
STRUCTURAL ENGINEER Peter Culley
CONTRACT VALUE $10 million
SIZE 150,000 square feet (14,000 square metres)
ACCESS limited

David Baker Associates 1990

David Baker Associates 1990

Post International

The Post International is a recognisable descendant of the International Style. Its fourteen storeys are distinguished by the fact that twelve of them are lifted off the ground on pilotis. These structural concrete columns are expressed both inside and out and are used to great effect to evoke the time when Modernism was chic. A curved curtain wall of tinted glass, that could have stepped straight out of the 1950s were it not partly over-laid in Late Modern fashion by a gypsum-based wall system, is the other dominant feature.

Together with a low-rise section that branches off the tower, the Post International consists of 72 units, none of them cheap. If unreconstituted Modernism can sell penthouse units for somewhere in the vicinity of $1.5 million, there must be life in the old dog yet.

ADDRESS 1388 Gough Street, SF 94109 [SF/A/CC SF 6 B2]
ARCHITECTS OF RECORD McNulty, Briskman & Heath
CLIENT O Interests
STRUCTURAL ENGINEER Bijan Florian & Associates
CONTRACT VALUE $19 million construction costs
SIZE 166,400 square feet (15,500 square metres) gross
ACCESS none

Kobe O 1994

Kobe O 1994

Fillmore Center

The towers of the Fillmore Center provide San Francisco with some of its most interesting tall buildings. Their pitched roofs, bay windows and colourful façades are distinctive and highly visible. The transposition of such vernacular elements to large buildings is difficult, but DMJM have carried it off. The towers are part of a mixed-use retail and rental development based on an 8.95-acre site in the Western Addition Redevelopment Project Area. 1113 residential units are divided between five towers from nine to nineteen storeys with lower – five- and six-storey – buildings creating a less monumental streetscape. Twenty per cent of the units are set aside for low- to moderate-income earners, 30 per cent are rented at 'affordable' rents and the rest go at market rates.

The Center appears to be a rarity: architecturally distinguished mass housing. But problems remain. The feeling that the buildings do not relate intimately to the streets that they are on is pervasive. This is no doubt largely because so much of the retail space is still empty, but it also has a lot to do with the 'enclosed compound' nature of the design. Courtyard housing is a wonderfully rich architectural model, but on this scale it tends to sap vitality from its surroundings. The internal gardens, which by any standards are generously planted, are not an adequate replacement for a strong street orientation. And, no matter how good the architecture, 8.95 acres of themed structures is about 7 acres too many.

ADDRESS 1475 Fillmore Street, SF 94115 [SF/A/CC SF 6 B3]
CLIENT Fillmore Center Associates
STRUCTURAL ENGINEER DMJM and Watry Engineers
CONTRACT VALUE $127 million
SIZE 1.6 million square feet (150,000 square metres)
ACCESS limited

DMJM (Daniel, Mann, Johnson & Mendenhall) 1991

DMJM (Daniel, Mann, Johnson & Mendenhall) 1991

Amancio Ergina Village

Its size, strong articulation and 'abstracted vernacular' style make this an impressive development. There are 72 units of subsidised, moderate-income housing on 1.72 acres. The buildings line the better part of three sides of a block and ring small gardens and extensive surface parking. With so much street frontage they become a castle in the city. The Ellis Street elevation, in particular, has become something quite exotic. Especially enjoyable are the bay windows that start angled, become square and then sprout horns, and are crowned by heavy pergolas. Square windows make no attempt to mirror the proportions of traditional houses and act to confuse the buildings' scale.

Despite being softened by a row of trees, the elevation lacks something. The very high, narrow openings between the pairs of horned towers are dark and inhospitable; their security gates add menace. These gated stairs are an omnipresent feature of San Franciscan housing, but few are as unsettling as these. Most are wider, many are lined with marble, others have tiled steps, some even have vases of flowers on them, provided by residents. It is hard to imagine people lingering in Amancio Ergina's dark chasms or wanting to personalise them. Another feature that is less than perfect is the surface car parking that desperately needs extensive land-scaping. This, however, is a function of the low budget.

ADDRESS Ellis, Scott, O'Farrell Streets, SF 9411 [SF/A/CC SF 6 A3]
CLIENTS Amancio Ergina Village Incorporated and the San Francisco Redevelopment Agency
STRUCTURAL ENGINEER Shapiro Okino Hom & Associates
CONTRACT VALUE $4.2 million construction costs
SIZE 54,000 square feet (5000 square metres)
ACCESS none

Solomon, Inc. 1985

Beideman Place Townhouses

These eleven market-value townhouses emulate a San Franciscan tradition that places a cottage at the rear of a lot with a full-size house at the front, separated by a narrow alley. In this case six two-storey cottages sit behind five three-storey houses. Access to the row of smaller buildings is through a broad archway that dominates the front elevation. Garage parking occupies the entire ground level of the street-side houses and is oriented both on to the street and on to the arched entryway. Exaggerated and idiosyncratic interpretations of traditional detailing make for a characterful street elevation.

With densities that equal 55 units per acre, a 1:1 car parking ratio, an architectural style that is easily assimilated into the street and the successful melding of communal and private, Beideman Place is a strong model for other developments.

ADDRESS Beideman Place, Beideman Street, SF 94115 [SFF/A/CC SF 6 A3]
CLIENT Beideman Investment Group
STRUCTURAL ENGINEER Raj Desai Associates
SIZE 11,650 square feet (10,800 square metres) of liveable space; 2775 square feet (258 square metres) of garaging
ACCESS none

Solomon, Inc. in collaboration with John Goldman 1989

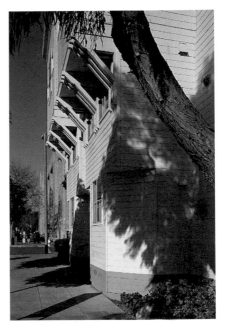

Solomon, Inc. in collaboration with John Goldman 1989

Cottage Row

Realising that it was pointless to try and match the grandeur of the neighbouring Victorian, the architects and their enlightened clients embarked on a scheme that would complement the older house without being overshadowed by it. For this rental apartment development, they decided to recreate the vigour and diversity of the San Francisco neighbourhood on a plot no bigger than 25 x 137.5 feet.

Mimicking a traditional San Franciscan building type, five townhouse apartments step back along the site, one behind the other, with access via a side yard. The individual units are each given their own character and what one sees from the street is a cluster of houses climbing over each other: a touch of Victorian here, a bit of Mediterranean there. There is the richness of historical vernacular without the cuteness of pastiche. There are also elements that are designed to grate: that seem too quirky or contrived. Why notch the parapet of the street wall, for example? Why make the immense corbels on the bay window asymmetrical? The answer, one feels, is partly just for the hell of it but also to create that element of dissonance that prevents complacent consumption.

Each unit is unique and although some are very small, great pains have been taken to maximise the feeling of space in each. Some have double-height living rooms with lofts, while all have some form of a view.

The houses sit on top of a five-car garage built with poured concrete and wood framing above.

ADDRESS 2910 California Street, SF 94115 [SF/A/CC SF 6 A2]
CLIENT Tom and Patty Landers
STRUCTURAL ENGINEER Barry Welliver
SIZE 550 square feet to 1100 square feet (51 to 102 square metres)
ACCESS none

Kotas/Pantaleoni 1986

Kotas/Pantaleoni 1986

San Francisco Waldorf School

The San Francisco Waldorf School (a Steiner school) is located in a very residential part of Pacific Heights. When the school wanted to expand it had to do so in as discrete a manner as possible. The original school buildings are low hipped-roof cottages and somehow the new buildings had to relate to these and to the surrounding Victorians.

The space the school was expanding into was occupied by a small supermarket. The architects raised the roof of this and converted it into a general-purpose hall with a foyer that opens onto the street, making it suitable for musical and stage performances as well as sports.

The curved roof trusses have been clad in ply which gives them an elegant but simple finish. A dance studio is located at the rear of the hall with a balcony that can be opened between the two. The studio is devoted to the study of eurythmy, a type of dance developed by Rudolph Steiner, and the building takes the form of a twelve-sided faceted dome, crowned by a glazed cupola.

Next to the hall, a three-storey classroom block faces the street. Its double-fronted bays could easily belong to a private residence and its well-proportioned elevation makes a suitable transition from the new structures to the old. Although highly contextual, this façade is rendered in a modern idiom with a skeletal cornice, tall rectangular windows that protrude from the curved bays and a wooden finish that could almost be painted poured concrete.

As this long, thin building extends into the site, it loses one level to the slope of the hill and loses half of its width to create a cloistered courtyard between itself and the older part of the school. A poured-in-place concrete elevator tower acts as a campanile and although this tower is rather overwhelming, the courtyard is delightful. A bridge that threatens to be engulfed by trumpet vine crosses between the old buildings and the

Tanner Leddy Maytum Stacy 1987

Tanner Leddy Maytum Stacy 1987

new, and the open space has been turned into a herb garden and a wonderful aviary constructed by the pupils from branches and wire mesh. (The school's headmaster describes the transition from the smaller older buildings where the younger children are taught to the larger, newer buildings as a movement from the village to the city.)

The courtyard and aviary are undoubtedly the heart of the school and hold the key to humanising the rather stern cloistered elevation. The concept of the cloisters is fine but its execution – particularly the very clunky blue-painted steel railings and stairs – is a little dated. The school should impose the medieval simplicity of its aviary on the rigid geometries of the cloisters, remove the ugly steel and replace it with bark-covered branches to accentuate the 'modern-primitivism'. Then they should let the trumpet vine run amok.

ADDRESS 2938 Washington Street, SF 94115 [SF/A/CC SF 6 A2]
CLIENT Henry S Dakin
STRUCTURAL ENGINEER Steven Tipping & Associates
CONTRACT VALUE $1.8 million construction
ACCESS none

Tanner Leddy Maytum Stacy 1987

Tanner Leddy Maytum Stacy 1987

Potrero Hill

MoST Building

Although this project was originally intended only as a simple light-industrial shed, the plan became more ambitious when the architects suggested that the owner/developer maximise his investment by putting apartments over the work element. The result is an extremely graceful building that is also a model for increasing the density of the city.

Smooth and split-faced concrete block is used on the ground floor while red stucco clads the residential second level. A classical motif is introduced by the pedimented façade but it is almost as easy to see a pair of agitated elephants in this elevation. (The concrete block around the two bays forms the legs. The four box bay windows that are grouped in pairs, angling away from each other over the bays, are the ears, while the two chimney flues are upturned trunks, trumpeting alarm.)

Potrero Hill

ADDRESS 80 Missouri, SF 94107 [SF/A/CC SF 11 B2]
CLIENT Segio Nibbi
STRUCTURAL ENGINEER Peter Tardos
SIZE 10,000 square feet (930 square metres)
ACCESS none

Kotas/Pantaleoni 1991

Potrero Hill

Kotas/Pantaleoni 1991

Gleeson Residence

Black asphalt shingles cover this house commissioned by two musicians. It is a sombre, misanthropic presence that is of deliberately indeterminate scale. It seems to stand on stilts and if you ignore its homely neighbours you could imagine it being an accommodation rig for North Sea oilmen, or an abbatoir or a prop for a science-fiction movie. It has style.

As a piece of architecture it is intriguing and provoking. As a neighbour it borders on being just plain rude – strange from one of San Francisco's most contextually sympathetic architects.

In plan it is U shaped, with two studio wings facing the garden. A skylit rotunda, housing a double spiral staircase, is at the centre of the building.

ADDRESS 610 Rhode Island Street, SF 94107 [SF/A/CC SF 11 B2]
CLIENT Pat Gleeson
STRUCTURAL ENGINEER Shapiro Okino Hom & Associates
SIZE 18,000 square feet (1700 square metres) and 575-square-foot (50-square-metre) garage
ACCESS none

Potrero Hill

Solomon, Inc. 1991

Solomon, Inc. 1991

18th and Arkansas

Potrero Hill is an area on the turn. Close to the fashionable South of Market district, on the doorstep of the proposed Mission Bay project but still a little down at heel, it is ripe for development. This project – on the site of an old railway tunnel – will offer a mix of housing ranging from 30 live/work lofts with one, two or three levels, to ten townhouses with either two or three bedrooms and 24 two-bedroom flats.

As is San Francisco's policy, a proportion of the units – 10 per cent in this case, or six lofts – will be made available at lower than market rates. People who qualify will be 'moderate income' earners (individuals who earn $48,400 or less, couples that make $55,300 or less). The inclusion of a second live/work loft scheme in the overall plan is noteworthy. This is being developed by an artists' organisation, Artsdeco, which was evicted from their SOMA (South of Market) building in 1983 by the Redevelopment Agency. Their portion of the project is designed to be rented at below market rates to working artists, with priority given to the original evictees.

The market-rate lofts occupy the 18th Street boundary of the site and are designed in an industrial aesthetic – a lot of metal siding is used – that is considered in keeping with the neighbourhood and attractive to the creative types who will buy them. Of course this whole notion is more of a marketing conceit than anything else, but architecturally it works. The block actually comprises four segments with a lot of variety within each to suggest a haphazard development over a period of time. Large windows provide great views and lots of natural light and the relatively narrow apartments are given interesting internal angles because the access stairs are skewed away from the orthogonal. Stucco of varying colours is used at ground level, balconies are given to some apartments and glazing patterns are not used repetitively.

David Baker and Associates 1994/1995

Potrero Hill

Potrero Hill

David Baker and Associates 1994/1995

The townhouses step up the hill along Arkansas in a similarly vernacular fashion and the Artsdeco segment is located within the two arms of this L shape along with a landscaped garden.

All in all this appears to be an innovative and appealing development – although a rather depressing sign of the times when a 1000-odd square-foot 'artist's loft' sells for somewhere between two and three hundred thousand dollars.

ADDRESS 18th and Arkansas, SF 94107 [SF/A/CC SF 11 B2]
CLIENT McKenzie Rose Holliday
STRUCTURAL ENGINEER Peter Culley
CONTRACT VALUE $11 million
SIZE 115,610 square feet (10,740 square metres)
ACCESS none

Potrero Hill

David Baker and Associates 1994/1995

Potrero Hill

David Baker and Associates 1994/1995

Spike & Spin

With a tall, rather elegant, fire station on the uphill side of this site and a small two-storey house on the downhill side, the architects were presented with the problem of how their building could relate to both sides at the same time.

The solution was to emulate the height and elegance of the fire station while dipping their design's roof down toward the lower structure, with a galvanised chimney flue on this lower corner acting like a stake to pin the slanting roof down. As they have done with other projects, the architects did everything they could to maximise the view from this building. There is a rotation within the building that shifts the alignment of the house so that instead of merely facing its neighbours, the façade is pulled apart and skewed toward the downhill view. This elevation is dominated by a considerably oversized window that both confuses the scale of the work and allows one to glimpse the tall spaces within.

Final touches include a curvy balcony, a lot of yellow paint and a splendid spiky flax by the black garage door.

Potrero Hill

ADDRESS 782 Wisconsin Street, SF 94107 [SF/A/CC SF 11 B3]
CLIENT K/P and COD Builders
STRUCTURAL ENGINEER Werner Martin
ACCESS none

Kotas/Pantaleoni 1991

Kotas/Pantaleoni 1991

The Mission to
Diamond Heights

The Slow Club

Exposed steel earthquake bracing, a low ceiling and a particularly hard-edged use of materials give this bar and restaurant a sci-fi, bunker-esque feel. Located on the ground floor of an old brick-built industrial building, the bracing is far from frivolous but the architects have taken it and made menacing sculpture of it. A black concrete floor and more raw steel in the form of bannisters and rails give the room a sombre feel that bright orangey-red Finn Color plywood panels only highlight. Bare cement walls, metal-framed windows and etched glass all add to the ambience of precision-menace while a velvet curtain over one wall hints that Dennis Hopper and Isabella Rossellini may not be far away.

ADDRESS 500 Hampshire Street, SF 94110 [SF/A/CC SF 11 A2]
CLIENTS Steven Decosse, James Moffet
STRUCTURAL ENGINEER Mike Kaszpurenko
CONTRACT VALUE $150,000
SIZE 12,000 square feet (1000 square metres)
ACCESS open

Praxis Architects 1992

The Mission to Diamond Heights

Praxis Architects 1992

Universal Café

Be sure to check out the Probat coffee roaster behind the curving marble counter at the Universal Café. It winks at you. An amiable fat boy, it has the charm of Thomas the Tank Engine.

The white marble of the counter, run through with blue cheese veins, meanders almost the full length of the room, gently curving to encourage the people sitting at it to face each other and chat. The room is a store dating from 1925 that has been given a coat of white paint and some exceptionally well-detailed but unobtrusive features. The counter, for example, is supported by steel 'pylons' anchored to concrete stanchions, that carry the marble like a bridge. Finn Color plywood panels are then screwed to this framework, creating a warm band of colour that is mirrored by the bench seat made of the same ply running along the opposite wall. Stools and chairs made specifically for the café unite the elements of wood and metal.

The street wall is made up of steel-framed windows that swing completely open on a satisfyingly robust hingeing mechanism that nevertheless hardly impedes one's view.

The front door is painted a bright blue and decorated with a red star, contrasting with the muted tones used inside. A canopy of steel and glass reminiscent of the Paris Métro runs the width of the façade.

ADDRESS 2814 19th Street at Bryant, SF 94110 [SF/A/CC SF 11 A2]
CLIENT Robert Voorhees
SIZE 1400 square feet (130 square metres)
ACCESS open

The Mission to Diamond Heights

South Park Fabricators 1993

The Mission to Diamond Heights

South Park Fabricators 1993

Urban Eyes Optometry

Urban Eyes sells glasses in the front of the store and has a lab and examining rooms at the back. Glasses are displayed against the two side walls, one covered by a perforated metal screen that allows glimpses of rough concrete columns, the other a smooth stucco finish, broken into bays by columns that translate into beams and cross the ceiling. A sinuous wooden platform extends from this wall while the rest of the floor is finished in bands of coloured linoleum.

Chairs and tables, designed by the architect, encourage people to take their time and to sit and linger. A desk of matching maple veneer is situated next to a staircase that leads to the mezzanine floor. A random steel rod bannister injects an aspect of diffuse energy into the otherwise controlled atmosphere. A bas-relief eye cut into the upper wall allows observation from the mezzanine.

ADDRESS 2253 Market Street, SF 94114 [SF/A/CC SF 10 B2]
CLIENTS Drs Albert C Lee and Lawrence Tom
CONTRACT VALUE $120,000
SIZE 1000 square feet (90 square metres)
ACCESS open

John Lum Architect 1993

John Lum Architect 1993

348 Church Street

Unlike many apartment or condominium projects which try to blend in with their neighbours, this structure takes 'vernacular' at face value and does whatever it wants. The most notable feature is the way it quite happily spreads horizontally. The architect wanted to create a horizontal energy that could be appreciated from the streetcar that runs down Church Street. Bays are angled projections linked by broad sweeps of balconies and the whole thing is topped by a curved cornice. Original computer-graphic projections for the paint scheme showed hot pinks, pastel blues, bright yellows, inky blues and light greys, but the building has ended up in anodyne shades of beige.

The Mission to Diamond Heights

ADDRESS 348 Church Street, SF 94114 [SF/A/CC SF 10 B2]
CLIENT Matt Murphy
STRUCTURAL ENGINEER Santos & Urrutia
SIZE 26,293 square feet (2440 square metres)
ACCESS none

Gary Gee Architecture 1995

Gary Gee Architecture 1995

The Mission to Diamond Heights

Harris/Foster House

The tall curved bays on this pair of houses, topped by the railings of their flat roofs give these structures a Moderne feel. The houses are clad in cement board – perhaps its first use for such a purpose in the Bay Area, although it is now a commonplace, particularly in Oakland's fire zone. (But note, Bernard Maybeck used an asbestos board in his First Church of Christ, Scientist in Berkeley in 1910.) A grid of extruded aluminium secures the board in place, giving a clean, rigorous appearance.

Interiors are equally spare. Living spaces open onto a steel-tread staircase which ascends in short flights the full height of the house to an electronically retractable skylight. A small fish pond sits at the foot of the stairs to create an elemental trajectory from water to sky. Materials are used simply and directly and there is a Japanese confidence in their unadorned expression.

ADDRESS 333 Cumberland Street, SF 94114 [SF/A/CC SF 10 B3]
CLIENT Michael Harris
STRUCTRUAL ENGINEER Cevet Kepkep
SIZE 2400 square feet (223 square metres)
ACCESS none

Michael Harris Architecture 1988

The Mission to Diamond Heights

Michael Harris Architecture 1988

Del Carlo Court

Army Street is one of the Mission District's major east–west thorough-fares. Capp Street is a narrow, north–south street that dog-legs and terminates at Army. In the almost triangular site between these two streets is Del Carlo Court: three low-rise blocks built around a courtyard, containing 25 low-income rental units.

A flat, barn-like façade faces Army Street, marked by over-sized eaves and huge brackets. It is broken by a large, deep entryway that heightens the impression that this could be a garage or a hay barn. The first three floors are given a clapboard effect while the top floor is in a board and batten style. Cream, brown and white paint are used throughout. A similar elevation looks on to Capp Street.

Units come with one, two, three or four bedrooms and two apartments are set aside for handicapped residents. Solomon's elegant solution to the nightmare of providing parking on a 1:1 ratio is to cluster the garages around the two entryways.

At present 87 people live in the Court and by all accounts it is a well-liked and desirable place to live. The dilapidated public housing projects further down Army Street are sad evidence that architecture does not easily solve society's problems, but you can't help thinking that more developments like Del Carlo Court might help.

ADDRESS 3330 Army Street, SF 94110 [SF/A/CC SF 14 C1]
CLIENT Mission Housing Development Corporation
STRUCTURAL ENGINEER Peter Culley & Associates
CONTRACT VALUE $3.5 million construction
SIZE 41,491 square feet (3855 square metres) gross
ACCESS none

Solomon, Inc 1993

Solomon, Inc 1993

Building at Mission and Army Streets

On a corner site at the intersection of Mission and Army Streets is one of San Francisco's wilder concoctions. The one-time home of the Doggie Diner now hosts three separate buildings that look as if they just might be one. They are, in fact, the work of three different architects who were actually at pains to avoid collaboration in order to create a genuinely vernacular grouping.

The corner element, a blaze of red stucco, is by Kotas/Pantaleoni. The middle element, a firework display that shoots everywhere at once, is by Garry Gee. The final element, a demure and sensible punctuation mark to the preceeding frivolity, is by Team 7.

The K/P piece is a lipstick tower that wraps the corner of these two major streets in a fashion that takes the term 'Barraganesque' way beyond the often overly respectful copying of colourful planes and stark court-yards. This building is in motion. The sliced cylinder of the tower sends one's eyes skyward as do the rows of stepped windows that mirror a stairway and the peaked cut-outs of the retail spaces on the ground floor. Above these, in a band of green stucco topped by a cornice line, the windows of second-floor offices follow a syncopated rhythm.

The final element is a cream-coloured block of town houses, their three window bays stepping out from the plane of the building like formation dancers.

ADDRESS 1300 Mission Street, SF 94110 [SF/A/CC SF 14 C1]
CLIENT The Evans Company
STRUCTURAL ENGINEER V/K Engineering
SIZE 4500 square feet (420 square metres) commercial, four two-storey townhouses of 850 square feet (80 square metres) each
ACCESS to retail

Kotas/Pantaleoni 1991

Kotas/Pantaleoni 1991

3405 Army Street

The programme called for three walk-up apartments over garage and office space. Two separate entrances on either side of the lot serve the different functional areas with a large banded archway leading to the offices and a more discrete set of pilasters marking the stairs to the apartments on the third and fourth levels. Curved balconies push out from a riot of broken arches and columns. Wild colours give the façade an extra jolt.

This looks like PoMo on hallucinogens, but the design actually alludes to Tibetan architectural features. The deep fenestration, rusticated openings, colour used to accentuate door and window openings, even the 'ears' at the top of each side of the building, all make passing reference to Tibetan forms.

ADDRESS 3405 Army Street, SF 94110 [SF/A/CC SF 14 C1]
CLIENT Marshmellow Corporation
STRUCTURAL ENGINEER V/K Engineering
SIZE 6188 square feet (575 square metres)
ACCESS none

Gary Gee Architecture 1991

Gary Gee Architecture 1991

One-O-Two Laidley Tansev House

Built as a speculative venture by Kotas and Pantaleoni, 102 Laidley is actually more restrained than a straightforward commission might have been. The need to recoup their investment led to a degree of caution that an observer unfamiliar with K/P's work might find hard to identify. The project alludes to the Bay Area tradition in its use of cedar shingles but then spices things up in a decidedly untraditional way. A window emerges from the house at an angle, pushing, it seems, a semi-circular balcony before it while, at a lower level, a white picket fence is revealed behind a stucco wall. A fence of vivid blue palings which do not quite align shields a staircase. An ungainly structure supports the balcony. Elements have been brought together in a way that might appear only arbitrary, and there certainly is a wilfulness to the design, but the intention is to create a structure that does not lend iteslf to a single interpretation: one that creates levels of potential meaning and encourages the participation of the observer.

Pragmatic considerations mix with a desire to embrace traditional forms in a modern context. The window is skewed toward the view. The picket fence evokes an idealised suburban past. The blue stairs refer to the restaurant at Sea Ranch. Roof trusses are left exposed partly because they look good and partly because it is cheaper that way.

ADDRESS 102 Laidley Street, SF 94131 [SF/A/CC SF 14 B2]
CLIENT K/P
STRUCTURAL ENGINEER Samuel Schneider
SIZE 1800 square feet (170 square metres)
ACCESS none

Kotas/Pantaleoni 1987

Kotas House

Looking more like a hippie shack in Costa Rica than an architect's house in San Francisco, this unlikely structure, laden with bougainvillea and thunbergia, combines high spirits and a low budget with learned references. Externally it is little more than a plywood box, with the ply cut to resemble monumental masonry and painted an electric blue and a now-faded red inspired by primative Mexican folk art. The arched window that is cut into this box is overlaid with a crude balcony, painted bright orange and yellow that gives the house the look of the setting sun. A Looney Tunes fence that undulates down to a little gate defines the plot.

The 1700-square-foot house is divided into three floors although the top two are fundamentallly one large open space. Arches inspired by Greek Byzantine churches rise the full height of these two storeys and a circular cut-out unites the levels.

ADDRESS 123 Laidley Street, SF94131
[SF/A/CC SF 14 B2]
CLIENT Jeremy Kotas
STRUCTURAL ENGINEER Joshua B Kardon
SIZE 1700 square feet (158 square metres)
ACCESS none

Jeremy Kotas 1983

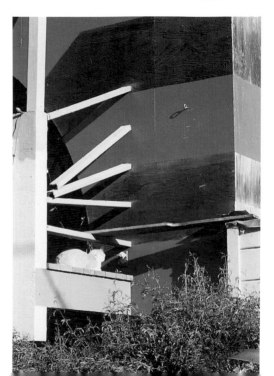

Gregory-Ingraham House

The Gregory-Ingraham House is known locally as the 'Owl House' and by the architects as the 'time machine'. The sloping site could not easily accommodate the typical rowhouse box so the architects split their form into two towers, square in plan and slightly twisted away from each other but linked by a more freely formed element. The first tower is clad in over-size 'Long John' redwood shingles, chosen to confuse the scale of the tall, three-storey structure. An enormous window provides views from the street to the atrium within, dominated by a wall of books. Topping off the façade are a pair of mouldings, like a curved pediment that has been broken and reversed. The door is surrounded by a decorative architrave – a pairing of rustic shingle and Georgian motifs in keeping with the early Bay Area tradition and the work of architects such as Ernest Coxhead.

The architects describe the procession through the interior as one through time as well as space. The low-ceilinged rooms that occupy the ground floor are painted in rich, dark Regency colours but these soon give way to a stairway that takes you up to a literally soaring space. The first tower is open from floor to ceiling; the second comprises two levels – one kitchen, one bedroom and bath – that are each open to the atrium space and accessed by stairs and bridges that seem to cling to the walls like mountain paths. Bare metal, roughly finished, twists alongside the stairs as bannisters, while maple floors are offset by fire-engine-red kitchen units. Hardly traditional, this interior is unashamedly theatrical.

ADDRESS 140 Laidley Street, SF 94131 [SF/A/CC SF 14 B2]
CLIENTS William Gregory and Richard Ingraham
STRUCTURAL ENGINEER Kers Clausen
SIZE 1600 square feet (150 square metres)
ACCESS none

Kotas/Shaffer 1989

Otsego Gardens

Otsego Gardens demonstrates the potential for increasing housing density in San Francisco without building high-rises and the way small-scale developments do not have to disrupt an established neighbourhood.

Set back from Otsego Avenue in a mid-block plot, the three townhouses share a driveway which in theory acts as a communal area. Unfortunately it looks a little too characterless to encourage neighbourliness and the movement of cars must make it relatively inhospitable. The houses are sold as individual plots and, despite their terraced appearance, are separated from each other by a 2-inch gap. This reduces home-owner association fees and provides each occupant with greater flexibility to modify their structure.

The line of houses is staggered to provide a sense of privacy, both front and back. Each house is long and narrow, the façade only wide enough to accommodate a single-car garage, the front door and a staircase. Two other rooms, most commonly used as bedrooms, each with access to the back garden, complete the ground floor. Piggybacked above these are the living room and kitchen and another bedroom and bathroom. Internally, the gabled roof line creates an unexpectedly high ceiling. Light is brought into the top floor both by skylights and by clerestory windows that express themselves in the front elevations as large square boxes, slung over the shoulder of each house.

ADDRESS Otsego Gardens (near Oneida Avenue), 438 Otsego Avenue, SF 94112 [SF/A/CC SF 20 A1]
CLIENT MacDonald & Nagle
STRUCTURAL ENGINEER Uno Veideman
SIZE 1200 square feet (110 square metres) each unit
ACCESS none

The Mission to Diamond Heights

MacDonald Architects 1992

MacDonald Architects 1992

Faith's House

Like a lifeguard on the beach at Venice, this house keeps its eye on the water. Perched on tiptoes above its garage, the main body of the house – a yellow ply construction – twists itself toward the Bay. You can see the energy the structure is exerting, almost feel the torque, as it strains toward the view. For once, the potential for plasticity that is inherent in California's wood-frame construction methods is being utilised. Oddly, though, although there is nothing really familiar about this house, there is nothing really alien about it either. It fits into its street like an Hawaiian shirt at a wedding: a little bright, a little unexpected, no doubt the subject of some whispered comments, but welcome nonetheless.

The interior is just as enjoyable. High ceilings, angled in all directions, and numerous skylights fill the sensuous spaces with light. White paint, maple floors, curved walls and an immaculate finish throughout make this house a delight.

(NOTE this project is located outside the immediate Mission to Diamond Heights area.)

ADDRESS 1539 Felton Street, SF 94134 [SF/A/CC SF 20 C1]
CLIENT Faith Gohstand
STRUCTURAL ENGINEER Werner Martin
SIZE 1800 square feet (170 square metres)
ACCESS none

Kotas/Pantaleoni 1991

Lincoln Park and Oceanside

Oceanside Water Pollution Control Project

This is part of San Francisco's combined sewer system which deals with both human effluent and storm-water. The plant is designed to reduce the discharge of pollutants into the ocean and the Bay. Before Oceanside came on-line even minor rainfall could cause failure in the antiquated system, with raw sewage being discharged into the sea and ending up on the beaches. Since Oceanside became operative, such overflows have been reduced by over 80 per cent.

Oceanside serves 380,000 people on San Francisco's west side and is designed to deal with a peak wet weather flow of 65 million gallons of combined waste and storm-water daily. The raw sewage arrives at the plant from the Westside Pump Station and it then goes through processes of screening, clarifying, aerating and bacteriological breakdown, before going to vast anaerobic digesters that act 'like giant stomachs'. Solids from the digesters either end up in landfill or on agricultural land while liquid waste is pumped 4 miles out into the ocean. Biogas produced in the digesters is used in the Energy Recovery Facility to produce electricity and hot water to heat the plant.

In designing the plant, the engineers and architects were charged with making it as clean, quiet, odour-free and inconspicuous as possible. Not only that, the plant also had to share its location with the San Francisco Zoo. Oceanside is just to the south of the zoo and one of the determining factors in siting the plant there was the assurance that the future expansion of the zoo would be catered for. The architects' solution to this unusual programme was to bury as much of the works underground as possible and to push the exposed facilities to the southern-most point of the site. Seventy per cent of the facility is underground and 6 acres of the site will be shared with the zoo. The roof of the underground portion is

Lincoln Park and Oceanside

Simon Martin-Vegue Winkelstein Moris 1994

Simon Martin-Vegue Winkelstein Moris 1994

designed to take a 300-pounds-per-square-foot live load to accommodate the drainage rock, soil, trees and animals that will eventually be placed on it. The exposed facilities are located in a man-made canyon that shields them from the surrounding beaches and roads and the most anyone is likely to see of the project is the entry tunnel that leads into the canyon.

The architects conceptualised this space as a natural element created by the flow of water, like a gorge or river valley, and have gone some way to humanising the scale of the monumental concrete retaining walls by horizontally banding them to evoke natural strata, while motifs of water flow are also included. It seems unnecessary. The pure drama of driving through the tunnel into this hidden valley does not need to be mediated in any way. The bulbous, onion-shaped domes of the digesters, with their catwalks and spiral staircases, or the labyrinthine and cavernous underground chambers, are more than adequate testament to the power of purely functional industrial design.

ADDRESS 3500 Great Highway, SF 94132 [SF/A/CC SF 12 A3]
CLIENT San Francisco Department of Public Works
ENGINEER CH$_2$M Hill
CONTRACT VALUE $220 million
SIZE plant, 7 acres (3 hectares) on 12-acre (5-hectare) site
ACCESS call 415 431 9430 for information

Simon Martin-Vegue Winkelstein Moris 1994

Lincoln Park and Oceanside

Lincoln Park and Oceanside

Simon Martin-Vegue Winkelstein Moris 1994

California Palace of the Legion of Honor

The California Palace of the Legion of Honor is a three-quarter-scale copy of the French original, used as an art museum. It has recently reopened after seismic retrofitting and expansion. Most of this expansion was downwards, with a new gallery space located below the central courtyard and lit by a pyramidal skylight. The obvious comparison with Pei's work at the Louvre must have been daunting for the architects, not least because the Legion of Honor is a fraction the size of the Louvre. This does create a problem. The skylight was never going to be a grand gesture and it isn't. It makes you think that anything apart from a pyramid would have been better, just to avoid that unfair comparison. A circular oculus, flush-mounted glass panels, anything but a pyramid. Anything but the bulky spotlights used inside the gallery, too, which severely clutter the ceiling.

Having said that, the way the design opens up three sides of the new lower level to the exterior, rather than just leaving them buried in the hillside, is inspired. Equally, the difficult retrofitting is invisible to the visitor and the stark symmetries of the colonnaded courtyard and façade are treated with a justified reverence.

ADDRESS 100 34th Avenue, Lincoln Park, 34th Avenue at Clement Street, San Francisco 94121
CLIENT The Fine Arts Museums of San Francisco
GENERAL CONTRACTOR Hensel Phelps Construction Company
STRUCTURAL ENGINEER GFDS Engineers
SIZE 125,000 square feet
COST $36.5 million
ACCESS open

Lincoln Park and Oceanside

Mark Cavagnero Associates

Edward Larrabee Barnes/John M.Y. Lee Architects 1995

Emeryville and Berkeley

US Postal Station, Emeryville

After years of neglect, the Postal Service is again sponsoring designs for their facilities that are more than bland boxes. The Emeryville station is an example of how a thoroughly functional programme can be spiced up.

The Post Office's immediate neighbours are railway tracks, with a new Amtrack station nearby, and a mix of warehouses and offices. In this context, and as the main requirement of the programme was a large space for sorting and dispatching mail, it is appropriate that a warehouse form was chosen. The strength and simplicity of this building type has some advantage and it has been personalised in ways that are strikingly photogenic. A curved-roofed volume, clad in corrugated metal siding and distinguished by five pairs of skylights or dormer windows, houses the sorting room. A lower section at the northern end of the site, animated by a canopy of brightly painted steel that leads clients from the parking lot to the entrance, houses the customer-service elements.

To keep work spaces as flexible as possible, employee facilities were pulled out of the main structure and are housed in a bright yellow stucco box that branches out from the main shed in the south-east corner. This is notable for the strongly geometric treatment of its masses and its five steeply sloping skylights. Another enigmatic appendage on this eastern elevation is a concrete cylinder with a menacing lookout gallery that marks one of the entraces to the sorting room.

ADDRESS 62nd Street, Emeryville 94608 [SF/A/CC Alameda 3 E5]
CLIENT United States Postal Service
STRUCTURAL ENGINEER Lawrence Fowler & Associates
CONTRACT VALUE $2.8 million
SIZE 20,000 square feet (1858 square metres)
ACCESS to Post Office

Emeryville Ratcliff Architects 1994

Emeryville Ratcliff Architects 1994

Hollis Street Project

Banta turns the usual practice of warehouse conversion on its head in these Emeryville offices. Most projects of this type turn their backs on the outside world and create a world of imagination within a protective carapace, but here the architect invites the world inside.

The old building has been stripped back to its bones, the concrete pillars left exposed and then in-filled with walls of glass. The long, low elevation on Hollis Street is ordered and controlled and offers another of the architect's redefinitions of the future by suggesting that the dystopia most warehouse refurbishments hint at may not materialise.

Emeryville and Berkeley

ADDRESS 5900 Hollis Street, Emeryville 94608 [SF/A/CC Alameda 3 E5]
CLIENT Hollis Street Project Partnership
STRUCTURAL ENGINEER Joshua B Kardon
CONTRACT VALUE $5.4 million
SIZE 125,000 square feet
(11,610 square metres)
ACCESS open

Philip Banta Architecture 1988

Philip Banta Architecture 1988

Folger/Murray Office/Warehouse

The straightforward box of this flexible office/warehouse has been pulled apart at its midsection to create a recessed entry. The businesslike metal siding gives way to fiesta-coloured doors and windows and a sweeping balcony. (Or at least they used to be fiesta coloured. At the time of writing, the red doors, blue windows and yellow balcony had all been painted a miserable grey.) A ramshackle roof over the balcony continues the ebullience of this tongue-in-cheek vision of the post-industrial landscape.

Emeryville and Berkeley

ADDRESS 1020 Folger Avenue, Emeryville 94710 [SF/A/CC SF 3 E3]
CLIENT Folger/Murray Properties
STRUCTURAL ENGINEER Nellie Ingraham Associates
CONTRACT VALUE $90,000
SIZE 3900 square feet (360 square metres)
ACCESS none

Philip Banta Architecture 1989

Philip Banta Architecture 1989

Tang Center

The Tang Center, part of UC Berkeley's University Health Service, provides out-patient care and a range of other services to more than 50,000 people, the bulk of whom are Cal's 31,000 students.

The three-storey centre is divided into two wings linked by a full-height atrium lobby. A total of 32 departments in eight service areas occupy the building, with the highest traffic departments located on the ground floor and the lowest on the third.

The project was divided into four bid packages to allow fast-track construction methods to be used: in other words, while the public areas were being built the clinical spaces were still being designed.

The building mediates between university and town. Most visitors arrive on foot, and a non-institutional, pedestrian-oriented design was arrived at. Spreading roofs with broad overhangs top the Clerical and Administrative wings with the heavily glazed lobby uniting the two. Natural ventilation not only helped to keep costs down, but the absence of ducts meant that the roof line could be kept lower and the scale of the building reduced. Concrete shear walls that dominate the ground level give way to curtain walls above, with the third level creating a *piano nobile* effect.

ADDRESS 2222 Bancroft Way, Berkeley 94720 [SF/A/CC Alameda 2 C7]
CLIENT University of California
STRUCTURAL ENGINEER Forell/Elsesser Engineers
CONTRACT VALUE $18 million
SIZE 75,000 square feet (6970 square metres) gross
ACCESS limited

Emeryville and Berkeley

Anshen + Allen 1992

Anshen + Allen 1992

Main Library Complex, University of California Berkeley

This project involved the seismic upgrading of the well-liked Doe Library, a 1912 Beaux Arts granite building, and the not-so-well-liked Moffitt Library, a 1968 Modernist concrete building, and their linking by a 180,000-square-foot underground addition. The addition houses the Main Library's 900,000 central volume collection and will allow for expansion to 2 million volumes.

With Berkeley's shrinking open spaces, the decision to go underground was probably the only way to accommodate such a large structure. Certainly no-one would have wanted to lose any part of the lawns around University Drive, considered one of the campuses most attractive spaces. The architects were anxious to minimise the impact of their building on this area and so, where the roof does manifest itself on the surface, they have created a Beaux Arts terrace that looks as if it could have been part of Doe's original design.

If the architects ever felt frustrated at not being able to express their work above ground, they have channelled all their energies into making spectacular spaces below it. Handled in a vocabulary of 'Expensive Modern', the spaces are polished in all senses of the word. Grandest of the grand gestures is the spiral staircase that forms the central circulation core of the addition.

ADDRESS UC Berkeley, Berkely 94720 [SF/A/CC Alameda 2 C6]
CLIENT University of California
STRUCTURAL ENGINEER Rutherford & Chekene
CONTRACT VALUE $36 million construction
SIZE 186,000-square-foot (17,280-square-metre) addition
ACCESS none

Emeryville and Berkeley

Esherick Homsey Dodge & Davis 1995

Esherick Homsey Dodge & Davis 1995

Life Sciences Building Addition, University of California Berkeley

The Life Sciences Addition claims to defer to the surrounding classical buildings by using similar materials, colours and forms but the result is something quite individual. A terracotta tile roof somewhat incongruously tops MBT's abstract rendering. An entrance is set back into the volume, overlaid by a structural grid. Top-floor windows alternate between square and round, creating a horizontal emphasis. Other windows – rectangular with gridded crowns – emphasise verticality. The effect is of a thin façade, like cut and folded paper, that is lightly applied to enclose the volume of the building.

This building was the first structure on the Berkeley campus to use fast-track construction methods.

Emeryville and Berkeley

ADDRESS UC Berkeley, Berkeley 94720
[SF/A/CC Alameda 2 C6]
CLIENT University of California
STRUCTURAL ENGINEER Forell/Elsesser
Engineers
CONTRACT VALUE $37.7 million
SIZE 200,000 square feet (18,580
square metres)
ACCESS none

MBT Associates 1987

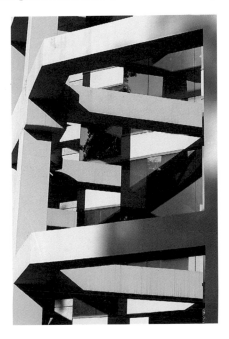

Emeryville and Berkeley

MBT Associates 1987

The Flora Lamson Hewlett Library

The Flora Lamson Hewlett Library was designed in the spirit of a conceptual design by Louis Kahn and it is not difficult to see Kahn's influence. The four-storey building is entered at the second level and book stacks and service functions are arrayed around a central atrium that rises three floors and drops one. An oculus has been cut between second and first levels to open the lower floor to the high square atrium. The best views in the library are from the lowest level where one looks up through the circular cut-out to the 3 x 3 grid of the square ceiling. Concrete structural elements are left exposed and in-filled with wooden panels which soften the stark geometries of the design. If there is a quibble about the execution of the plan it is that the ring of display cases around the oculus on the second floor keeps one too far away from the opening and rather removes one from the full experience of it.

The exterior is intentionally undemonstrative with the mass dissolved through a series of set-backs in the form of tree-lined terraces that provide seating from which the spectacular views can be enjoyed.

Emeryville and Berkeley

ADDRESS 2400 Ridge Road, Berkeley 94709 [SF/A/CC Alameda 2 C6]
CLIENT Graduate Theological Union
ASSOCIATED ARCHITECTS Peters Clayberg and Caulfield
STRUCTURAL ENGINEER Rutherford & Chekene
CONTRACT VALUE $8 million construction
SIZE 50,000 square feet (4645 square metres)
ACCESS limited

Esherick Homsey Dodge & Davis 1987

Walter A Haas School of Business Administration

With some justification, the Haas Business School has already been compared to a Bavarian hotel. Moore Ruble Yudell, like William Turnbull in his Foothill Student Housing, have adopted the vocabulary of wooden house construction used in the vicinity and applied it to a much larger structure. And one made out of concrete. The concrete walls have been formed to create the look of board and batten and clapboard and they have been painted in a rather sombre range of greens and browns and creams. Dormer windows interrupt the large expanses of sloping roofs while two semi-circular gateways serve as entrances to the complex.

Regardless of what one thinks of the style of this building, one has to admire the guiding principles of the architecture. The programme has been divided to allow the creation of three linked buildings which are grouped around a 'dry creek' that meanders down the hillside creating a central open space that takes the form of a series of stepped gardens or a linear courtyard. The heart of the design is what the architects describe as a 'student forum' featuring an open area backed on to by a series of stairways that will double as seating. The design aims to create impressive spaces that maintain a human scale and encourage interaction.

ADDRESS UC Berkeley, Berkeley 94720 [SF/A/CC ALAMEDA 2 D7]
CLIENT Walter A Haas School of Business UCB
STRUCTURAL ENGINEER T Y Lin International
SIZE 220,000 square feet (20,440 square metres)
ACCESS none

Moore Ruble Yudell 1995

Moore Ruble Yudell 1995

Foothill Student Housing

Like his one-time partner Charles Moore, whose Haas Business School is nearby, William Turnbull has undertaken this large project for UC Berkeley in a spirit of contextuality. A respect for the vernacular is manifested in an eccentric form that takes familiar elements and gives them a slight twist. In this case the buildings which spread out on either side of Hearst Avenue end up looking like a Utah ski lodge. Green asphalt tiled roofs, cedar shingles and board and batten provide the background colours while cupolas, bark-covered redwood tree trunk columns and cantilevered cat-walks enliven the composition.

Although the Tyrolean entrance might not suit every palate, the buildings catch the sun well, handle their bulk comfortably and are inviting presences.

Again like the Haas Business School, the way the structures relate to open space is one of the architects' prime concerns. The buildings to the south of Hearst form a spine along the perimeter of the site, creating an extended courtyard garden between themselves and Stern Hall, another student building. The structures on the Hearst/La Loma block are more tightly packed and form a more urban series of courtyards stepping down the hillside and connected on the diagonal.

ADDRESS Hearst Avenue at La Loma/Gayley Road Berkeley 94710 [SF/A/CC Alameda 3 C5]
CLIENT University of California
STRUCTURAL ENGINEER SOH & Associates
CONTRACT VALUE $29 million
SIZE 252,000 square feet (23,400 square metres)
ACCESS none

William Turnbull Associates with The Ratcliff Architects 1991

William Turnbull Associates with The Ratcliff Architects 1991

Revenge of the Stuccoids

The name of this house comes from the way the boxy stucco elements visible from the street seem to have engulfed the more conventional pitched-roof volumes that in fact comprise a significant part of the structure. The architect explains his design as the point at which stucco houses from the flatlands battle with venerable hillside houses designed by Bernard Maybeck.

The first impression of the house is one of aloofness. A rather forbidding garage door dominates the ground level and the unrelenting grey stucco, a cyclopean tower and a spiked pergola create the image of a fortified retreat. Closer aquaintance reveals a path of stepping stones up to the deck which wraps around the house and French doors that open the living areas to the exterior. Once inside, the tensions continue: a kitchen of space-station frugality with appliances slung from steel posts faces the most conventional masonry fireplace one could imagine (although it is skewed away from the wall). Low sheetrocked ceilings in the dining and kitchen areas give way to a high cable-truss roof of stained timber. Simple stucco and cement work is contrasted with the work of artist-artisans such as Twyla Arthur, Jeff Sand and Paco Prieto.

Emeryville and Berkeley

ADDRESS 2997 Dwight Way, Berkeley 94704 [SF/A/CC ALAMEDA 2 D7]
CLIENTS Nancy Whitcombe and David Baker
STRUCTURAL ENGINEER Caveh Rad
CONTRACT VALUE $550,000
SIZE 2899 square feet (269 square metres)
ACCESS none

David Baker Associates 1993

West Oakland and Emeryville

Marcus Garvey Commons

Like its near neighbour Independence Plaza, Marcus Garvey Commons could be accused of having too sunny a disposition: its architecture of green gabled roofs and pastel clapboard seems to have a Pollyanna sentimentality at odds with its proximity to the elevated BART line, industrial buildings and semi-derelict houses. However, a case can be made that this optimistic, nostalgic blend is precisely the architecture that the area needs: renewal in a recognisable, even symbolic form. Metal-clad lofts might be fine for middle-class bohemians, but things are different here.

On a symbolic level the most important element in this design is the picket fence. Quite ludicrous in many ways, it is the fulcrum of the design in others. Evidently not a security device, it defines private space while never divorcing the houses from the street or the greater neighbourhood. The fence is there to outline the small gardens which, it is to be hoped, will soon be cultivated by the residents. It is a gesture of community that may well be nostalgic.

Twenty-two units line the street. Each family has its own patio front and back. Car parking is behind the houses and a community centre with a hipped roof and cupola faces the courtyard garden.

Density is 30 units per acre; costs are $62.70 per square foot.

ADDRESS 1753–1779 Goss Street, corner of Wood, West Oakland 94607 [SF/A/CC Alameda 7 D4]
CLIENT Jubilee West & East Bay Asian Local Development Corporation
STRUCTURAL ENGINEER Robert Ost Engineering
CONTRACT VALUE $1.4 million construction
SIZE 22,800 square feet (2200 square metres)
ACCESS none

Pyatok Associates 1992

Pyatok Associates 1992

Independence Plaza

Independence Plaza has all the spriteliness of a hotel at a Disney resort with its colourful buildings grouped around interconnected courtyard gardens. Two-, three- and four-storey buildings are finished in bands of blue-grey clapboard below cedar shingle, picked out by white window casings and blue bargeboards. Grey cement tiles are used on the hipped roofs and service towers are topped by navy blue sheet-metal. Roughly finished balconies of trellising or palings are painted white. The only incongruous feature is the high steel railing fence that rings the site.

The Plaza is in fact a mix of affordable and market-rate rental housing for senior citizens. This is not a nursing home – it is an 'independent care complex' where residents must be physically able to look after themselves or able to afford to employ whatever assistance they need. Increasing infirmity is catered for in the design, however, in that all the units are adaptable to wheelchair use, allowing residents to stay in their own apartments as their physical abilities decline. Preference for the affordable units is given to people who have been made homeless, are living in substandard housing or are paying more than 50 per cent of their income in rent.

In this context the architecture seems entirely appropriate: friendly and unintimidating in scale, finished in warm materials that evoke vernacular domestic architecture, protected and inward-looking. Unfortunately, the surrounds are rather desolate, and no sense of community exists.

ADDRESS 703 Atlantic Avenue, Alameda 94501 [F/A/CC Alameda 11 A2]
CLIENT Housing Authority of the City of Alameda
STRUCTURAL ENGINEER G-N-G Engineers
CONTRACT VALUE $10 million
SIZE 169,198 square feet (15,720 square metres)
ACCESS none

Kodama Associates 1990

Kodama Associates 1990

Oakland

Leviathan

Wonderfully irreverent, this commercial building is described by the architects as a supertanker entwined by a giant octopus, a conceit that is, given the dockside setting, 'contextual'.

The boxy stern of the supertanker is clad in a red and white chequer-board pattern of corrugated steel siding that is regularly punctured by square windows. The bow of the stricken and broken-backed vessel is represented by an element that is covered by a flush skin of metal panels and horizontal strips of glazing. Topping off this sloping-sided structure is a steel gangplank, suitable for a demented Captain Nemo, supported by a tracery of steel members that overlays some of the windows, and the dome of a grain silo, that together represent the bulbous head and a trailing tenacle of the fabulous beast. A saw-toothed roofline of skylights forms the back of the monster and is finished in copper-clad asphalt shingles that, encouraged to oxidise by a wash of acid, have already taken on the deep-sea hue of verdigris. The architects' top-floor studio continues the theme with exposed ductwork and nonstructural steelwork creating the entrails and ribs of the creature's innards.

The building is both enjoyable and functional (apart from the difficulty of locating the appropriate entrance) and, among some bland neighbours, is a positive addition to a wonderful working neighbourhood.

As an antidote to historicist pastiche, Leviathan already earns its keep, and as a reflection of the heroic scale of the enormous cranes and towering ships with their stacked containers, it very nearly holds its own.

The danger of such an imaginative and allusive approach to architecture is that a building can become an often repeated one-liner that soon loses its bite and that the layers of meaning that might appear to exist – and that give a good building its resonance – are simply not there. This building avoids that fate but one feels that the architects walk a thin line.

Ace Architects 1990

Ace Architects 1990

Buildings that are inspired by ideas and stories are always 'explainable'. This is both the strength and weakness of projects such as this one: they are clever and witty concoctions, but perhaps for a building to be great the architect has to venture into the realm of the inexplicable.

For anybody wondering how such a building ever got through planning, Oakland had, unlike its neighbour across the Bay, a *laissez-faire* approach to architecture: it had no design review and no height limits at the time Leviathan was built.

Oakland

ADDRESS 330 2nd Street, Oakland 94607 [SF/A/CC Alameda 9 A6]
CLIENT Ace Architects
SIZE 10,000 square feet (930 square metres)
STRUCTURAL ENGINEER Steven Tipping & Associates
ACCESS none

Ace Architects 1990

Ace Architects 1990

Right Away Redy Mix

Designing a building in a concrete works must be a dream come true for any architect who has ever admired industrial architecture. True, HHPJ was only asked to create a dispatch and administration building, but it was still in the same yard as the concrete silo. It was also in the post-industrial landscape around Alameda Harbor, with its decaying monuments to industrialisation and massively engineered bascule bridges. HHPJ's response is, like any good industrial building, enigmatic, raw and somewhat menacing. In fact it looks more like the control centre for a nuclear test in the Arizona desert *circa* 1950 than anything else.

Two storeys high and constructed of concrete block and glass, the structure's primary function is to provide an elevated room from which the loading of trucks can be supervised. To ensure safety and efficiency the operatives must be able to see all of the yard. A central location with all-around visibility and protection from the intense glare of the sun was called for. HHPJ chose to glaze the operations centre extensively and to protect it with guillotine-like sunshades that are electronically adjustable within an exoskeleton that is cantilevered out from the second floor – not necessarily the simplest, cheapest or best means of keeping sun out of the workers' eyes, but surely the most stylish.

ADDRESS 410 Kennedy Street, Oakland 94606 [SF/A/CC Alameda 11 E3]
CLIENT Right Away Redy Mix Company
STRUCTURAL ENGINEER Walt Vorfeld with Steven Tipping & Associates
CONTRACT VALUE $350,000
SIZE 4000 square feet (370 square metres) gross
ACCESS none

Holt Hinshaw Pfau Jones 1989

Oakland

Oakland

Holt Hinshaw Pfau Jones 1989

City Center, Oakland

The original planning for City Center started in the 1960s and early 1970s and was designed to revitalise downtown Oakland by linking BART to a new office and shopping development. An enormous underground parking garage, which was to be the deck on which the rest of the project was built, was completed but not much more. When the project was revived in 1985, the new planners (IDG with Cesar Pelli as an occasional advisor) came up with a new approach. The superblock concept was junked, the previously closed 12th Street was reopened, and 13th Street, which would have disappeared in the megastructure, was reestablished as a pedestrian thoroughfare and as the defining axis of the project. Low buildings now group around 13th Street with taller structures pushed to the perimeter. An axis runs from BART's entrance plaza, through a square ringed by restaurants and a shopping promenade, between KMD's twin Federal Buildings and past a particularly successful parking structure by IDG, to finally terminate in the delightful Preservation Park. (Here sixteen turn-of-the-century houses, eleven of them rescued from demolition and moved to this site, have been restored and now serve as offices.)

The whole redevelopment covers twelve city blocks with various architects involved. IDG did the master planning and designed the buildings around the 13th Street pedestrian street. Other noteworthy structures are KMD's GSA Federal Buildings and Gensler's American President Companies tower at 111 Broadway.

ADDRESS City Center, Broadway and 13th Street, Oakland 94612
[SF/A/CC Alameda 9 B5]
CLIENT Bramalea Pacific Limited
CONTRACT VALUE $350 million (total)
ACCESS open

Oakland

IDG (and various architects) 1993

IDG (and various architects) 1993

1111 Broadway

It would be faint praise to say that the American President Companies tower uses reflective glass better than most: the curved wall of glass that looks out on to Broadway is simply beautiful. The glass shines like gasoline on the ocean, sometimes a dull shimmer, sometimes a colourful blaze. The top of the tower is handsomely defined by a row of eight columns that perhaps drew inspiration from the nearby 1212 Broadway, an equally fine building that dates back to 1906.

It is a considerable disappointment that the architects did not simply repeat this recipe on the rear of the building but instead opted for an anodyne and instantly forgettable pre-cast stone-clad set of stepped planes, only partly compensated for by the glazed 'conservatory' that houses pieces from the Oakland Museum's collection.

ADDRESS 1111 Broadway, Oakland 94612
[SF/A/CC Alameda 9 B5]
CLIENT Bramalea Pacific Limited
STRUCTURAL ENGINEER Skilling Ward
Barkshire Magnusson Inc.
SIZE 580,296 square feet (53,910 square
metres); 25 storeys
ACCESS limited

Oakland

Gensler and Associates 1991

Gensler and Associates 1991

GSA Federal Building

In order to ensure that this project came to Oakland, City officials donated a 3.3-acre plot to the US General Services Administration. The building now houses 26 state and federal agencies which will employ approximately 4000 staff. It is estimated that they will spend somewhere in the region of $3 million annually in the immediate area.

The project not only boosts the depressed Oakland downtown, it also transforms the skyline. The twin 18-storey towers, linked by a skybridge at the 13th and 14th floors, now dominate much of the east bay. Their pyramidal peaks thrust skyward but, unfortunately, their podgy bodies anchor them securely to the ground. Like SOM's 100 First Street Building in San Francisco, the GSA towers should be twice as tall to deal successfully with their bulk. The very domestic, almost square, windows do nothing to help achieve lift off.

The towers are faced in bands of white and gold limestone and the buildings have a definite retro look to them. Fine public spaces are provided by the 1-acre plaza and the 75-foot-high rotunda, and their continuation of the 13th Street axis is a sympathetic piece of urbanism.

(Note for earthquake watchers: the skybridge is designed to move like the rod of a crankshaft in a 'quake, allowing for both lateral and front-to-back motion.)

ADDRESS Clay Street at 13th, Oakland 94607 [SF/A/CC Alameda 9 A4]
CLIENT General Services Agency (GSA)
STRUCTURAL ENGINEER Cygna Group
CONTRACT VALUE $180 million
SIZE 1,050,000 square feet (97,550 square metres)
ACCESS limited

Oakland

Kaplan McLaughlin Diaz 1993

Oakland

Kaplan McLaughlin Diaz 1993

Frank G Mar Community Housing

'The Mar' is named for the late Reverend Frank Mar who initiated the project. It took over seven years to complete and involved two failed attempts to obtain sites elsewhere in Oakland. This is a low-income project located on the border of Oakland's Chinatown and downtown in an area that has lost housing stock over the years to commercial developments. The Mar goes some way to adjusting the balance.

The non-profit developer took over the previously derelict site from the city and built a 210-car garage on it which was then sold back to the city. 119 apartments were built above the garage and a series of retail stores line the street fronts. The complex occupies most of one city block.

To qualify for housing, residents' incomes must be 50 to 60 per cent of the area's median, although eight units are set aside for people in the 40 per cent range.

There is a family orientation to the housing, with three- and four-bedroom townhouses ringing the perimeter of the site and enclosing a small courtyard. The houses are two deep to the south and the west and are separated by narrow alleys.

A nine-storey tower, which is occupied by older residents, lines the northern edge of the site and gives the design its eye-catching presence. The tower faces the enormous Oakland Hotel, which fills an entire block and is eight storeys high, and is an appropriate response to the older building. Like the three-storey townhouses, the tower is topped by gabled roofs of bright green metal and the domestic roofscape, so high off the ground, is one of the most likable features of the structure. The tall tower with its cantilevered higher levels might have been oppressive without them. As it is, the roofs pull the tower and the townhouses together without homogenising a varied design. Eaves and gables of the pitched roofs alternate, while recessed balconies, which have been formed by

MacDonald Architects 1990

Oakland

MacDonald Architects 1990

scooping out a semi-circle from the eaves-side of the houses, break both the façades and the roof lines and are a particularly successful stylistic device.

Although apartments are small and the communal spaces could, as is always the case, be bigger, the individualistic elements in the architecture prevent any feeling of blandness or homogeneity.

ADDRESS 13th Street and Harrison, Oakland 94612
[SF/A/CC Alameda 9 B5]
CLIENTS East Bay Asian Local Development Corporation and Bridge Housing Corporation
STRUCTURAL ENGINEER Leong/Razzano & Associates
CONTRACT VALUE $12 million
SIZE 94,900 square feet (8820 square metres)
ACCESS none

Oakland

MacDonald Architects 1990

MacDonald Architects 1990

Barclay Simpson Sculpture Studio

When the California College of Arts and Crafts needed more space for its glass-blowing workshop and metal foundry, James Jennings provided the school with a light-industrial factory shed that uses unexceptional materials in exceptional ways.

Enough space for large-scale sculptures and for bulky kilns and annealing ovens was the prime requirement and a 2800-square-foot box was provided. A poured-concrete base acts as a plinth for a slim steel grid that encloses glass block walls. A row of steel vents that are opened and closed manually immediately above the concrete base gives the impression that the glass element is disconnected from the concrete and is floating free. Miesian corners further lighten the mass and at night the building dissolves into a shimmer of artificial light.

ADDRESS 5212 Broadway, Oakland 94618
[SF/A/CC Alameda 4 D6]
CLIENT CCAC
STRUCTURAL ENGINEER A J Miller
CONTRACT VALUE $600,000
SIZE 2800 square feet (260 square metres)
ACCESS none

Oakland

James Jennings Arkitekture 1992

James Jennings Arkhitekture 1992

Aceland

Close to the California College of Arts and Crafts, a small cluster of offices, shops and stores has been given a facelift and reconfigured into a brightly coloured Deco fantasy. The architects describe their stylistic allusions as Moroccan, early New England and Romanesque. Exaggerated details and vivid colours create a highly stylised and even slightly surreal grouping of three structures that branch out from a small open space extending from the sidewalk. Each building has a symmetrical façade, defined either by twin parapets or towers. One of the street-facing structures is painted deep red, the other bright yellow, while the third building, set back on the site, and with a new second floor, is a vivid pale blue, further animated at night by strips of neon. The vaguely Arabic domes that crown the chunky towers of this building are in fact silo tops. To create the luxuriant curves that are a feature of these structures, a system of plaster and mesh-covered styrofoam was used.

The architects also worked on the interiors: of particular note are Community Travel and ACME Mortgage. Community Travel features an aeroplane 'wing' that appears to slice through the office at ceiling height; ACME Mortgage is laid out in the form of a Monopoly board with individual workspaces in the shape of simplified houses grouped around the familiar Monopoly properties and exhortations to 'Go Directly To Jail'.

Another Ace project, the Chimes Block, which uses elephantine Arts and Crafts detailing, is across the street.

ADDRESS 5299 College Avenue, Oakland 94618 [SF/A/CC Alameda 4 D6]
CLIENT Ace Construction and Development
STRUCTURAL ENGINEER Sam Sarmiento
SIZE 30,000-square-foot (2790-square-metre) addition
ACCESS open during business hours

Ace Architects 1989

Oakland

Ace Architects 1989

Oakland Hills

Wayne Dinkelspiel House

The primary consideration for the owners of this property when rebuilding after the fire was that their new house should, unlike the old one, relate to the land. They wanted to lose the frightening balconies of a house on stilts and gain a garden. Instead of entering the new house at street level, the architects take you from the street, through a pergola beside the garage tower, down a set of steps to an intimate garden established on the hillside, and only then to the front door.

None of the drama of the location is lost, as the house is still oriented to the view and its three levels provide more than adequate height to see to the bay.

Walls are mainly stucco, but wooden board, coloured with full-bodied stains that give a deep but textured finish, are used to highlight a tower over the front door and one that extends from the living room/bedroom area. The whole composition has the pleasing complexity of a number of farm buildings lassoed together.

ADDRESS 971 Alvarado Road, Oakland 94704
[SF/A/CC Alameda 4 E1]
CLIENTS Frances Dinkelspiel, Gary Wayne
STRUCTURAL ENGINEER Ingraham-DeJesse
& Associates
SIZE 3800 square feet (350 square metres)
ACCESS none

Oakland Hills

Siegal & Strain Architects 1993

Siegal & Strain Architects 1993

Kayo House

The complexity of this project is hard to appreciate when one is actually in it, so smoothly do spaces flow from one to another. It is only when shown a sketch of the house that one sees how the different volumes collide with each other – 'like a Columbian slum', as the owner happily declares. The apparent free-for-all, with various towers and boxes jostling for space, creates a house of numerous levels grouped around a central stairway. Views are maximised, a number of small roof terraces are created and a conventional oblong room is almost impossible to find. What could be a maelstrom of hyperactivity, however, is, with its tightly controlled palette of colours and materials, a calm interior, while the steeply sloping site actually exposes little of the structure to passers-by.

Oakland Hills

ADDRESS 373 Gravatt Drive,
Oakland 94705 [SF/A/CC Alameda 4 E2]
CLIENTS Kenny Katsoff, Diana Yonkouski
STRUCTURAL ENGINEER Caveh Rad
SIZE 3980 square feet (370 square metres)
ACCESS none

David Baker Associates 1994

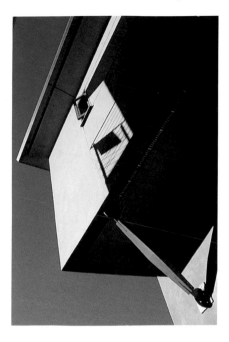

David Baker Associates 1994

Parsons Residence

Looking like a grazing tapir, this house extends from the hillside, its curved roof reflecting the slope of the terrain. Terraces step down the hill beside the house and link it to the exterior at a number of different levels. Concrete columns are left exposed in places but the structure is principally defined by the clean finish of cedar siding, detailed with extruded aluminium corner mouldings. The lack of distracting guttering or other protuberances emphasises the mass of the building and its flowing lines. Extensive glazing capitalises on the views while creating a bouyancy in the design.

ADDRESS 1111 Gravatt Drive, Oakland 94705 [SF/A/CC Alameda 4 E2]
CLIENTS Thomas and Barbara Parsons
STRUCTURAL ENGINEER Santos & Urrutia
SIZE 3332 square feet (310 square metres)
ACCESS none

Oakland Hills

Regan Bice Architects 1994

Walrod House

This house on the Berkeley/Oakland border marks the line where the 1991 fire was turned back. The original building was destroyed but it is possible to stand in the new house and look across the property-line to the mature and thriving gardens of houses opposite that were untouched by the flames. The division seems arbitrary and unjust.

The replacement house, however, exemplifies the area's spirit of hope and optimism maybe better than any other house in the fire zone. It quietly occupies its site and intimately integrates itself with the land. This isn't a house that shouts for attention, but one that is prepared to accept its place in the landscape.

Designs of almost child-like simplicity are set back from the street far enough to allow trees to be planted and for small courtyards to be established. The primary volume is a simple shed form that rises at one end into a tower. A bridge from this links to a secondary form, another tower. The framed space between the two, with views to the Golden Gate Bridge, is described as 'an offering to the public realm'. Surfaces are green-grey stucco, woodwork is picked out in dull yellows. The effect is self-effacing and reserved.

Once beyond the public domain, however, the house becomes more expansive and – marginally – more effusive. For once the cliché about a house that resembles an Italian hill town is accurate. The almost two-dimensional aspect that was presented to the street changes totally as the house takes on different heights and layers as it steps down the moderately sloped site and digs into the earth with terraces and intimate gardens.

The Italian town analogy holds good inside the house too, where it seems inappropriate to talk about rooms and corridors as these words do not come close to describing the feelings of spaciousness, movement

Oakland Hills

Moore Ruble Yudell 1994

Moore Ruble Yudell 1994

and surprise that the design engenders. A rich urbanism more readily comes to mind than any ideas of function and square footage.

The heart of the house is a broad passageway, off which high-ceilinged, modestly sized rooms gather on the street side of the structure. The passageway overlooks the garden, like an enclosed cloister, and eventually cascades down an equally broad staircase that, against all expectations, dead-ends. Off to one side, however, like a secret alley, is a narrow doorway that leads into a high room that in turn links with another room that opens out to the garden.

Oakland Hills

ADDRESS 225 Alvarado Road, Berkeley 94705 [SF/A/CC Alameda 4 E2]
STRUCTURAL ENGINEERS Dominic Chu, Mervin Dixon
SIZE 4800 square feet (4500 square metres)
ACCESS none

Moore Ruble Yudell 1994

Moore Ruble Yudell 1994

Drager House

Pug ugly the first time you see it, the Drager House grows on you. The fire zone is still a building site, however, and the structure feels exposed. Imagine it surrounded by tall trees, and the building becomes a much more sympathetic presence, an idiosyncratic beauty.

The exterior, with its copper carapace, defies conventional aesthetics and the interior does its best to keep pace. Rooms are mostly small and the emphasis is placed on connecting them in dramatic ways. Rooms at the front of the house, for example, on three different levels, are linked by a chasm hollowed out of the copper boomerang. This pulls light into each room from a high window but presumably will transfer sound from the first-level television room to the top-floor bedroom with even greater efficiency.

The house is simply contrary. It largely ignores the Bay view (which may be sensible given that no-one knows what will be built in the vacant lot on the Bay side of the house), it seems to go out of its way not to be a practical family home and it makes no concessions to conventionality. But the interiors are beautiful: full of canted walls and unexpected skylights and deep gorges. You get the feeling that this house is a maquette for Israel's Guggenheim Museum. Twenty times bigger and free of the mundanities of kitchens and bedrooms, the crystalline interiors will make a breathtaking art museum.

ADDRESS 160 Vicente Road, Berkeley 94705 [SF/A/CC Alameda 4 E2]
CLIENT Sharon Drager
STRUCTURAL ENGINEER Joseph Perazzelli
SIZE 3700 square feet (344 square metres)
ACCESS none

Oakland Hills

Franklin D Israel Design Associates 1994

Oakland Hills

Franklin D Israel Design Associates 1994

Laidley House

It is quite possible to overlook this house, already starting to be obscured by some lush planting and almost literally overshadowed as it is by the much more flamboyant Drager House across the way. Its willingness to blend into the background is the point and the house is noteworthy precisely for its undemonstrative nature.

Located on the downhill side of the street, its flat topped, stuccoed volume hardly detains one's eye as the more exuberant houses further down the street beckon. Only a curved element hints at any sort of complexity.

The real story is inside the building where an unreconstituted Modernism with Japanese overtones reigns. Rooms are universally painted white, sisal matting covers the floors and shoji screens divide rooms and cover windows. The curved wall manifests itself in the living areas and the lower bedroom and appears as a dramatic gesture in an otherwise strictly orthogonal plan and amid such simplicity. It is used to great effect in the living room where, together with a fireplace, it acts as the visual focus for the room. A concealed skylight throws a shaft of sunlight over the curve and on to the twin columns of the chimney flues. This is a nice reminder that light and the restrained manipulation of space can be all the dramatic effect one needs.

Oakland Hills

ADDRESS 151 Vicente Drive, Oakland 94705 [SF/A/CC Alameda 4 E2]
CLIENT Jane Laidley
STRUCTURAL ENGINEER B K Paul, Structural Engineer
SIZE 3800 square feet (350 square metres)
ACCESS none

James Gillam Architects 1994

XYZ House

Although this house is constructed like 90 per cent of the houses in the fire zone – with the standard components of wood frame, stucco and glass – it manages to look particularly machine-like. There is a seamless quality to its glazed wall that comes closer to the curtain walling of a large commercial structure than to anything one would usually expect in a one-family home. The blue tint of the glass, and the way its large expanse reflects so much of the sky, gives it an abstract, rather dreamy quality. This is the Machine Age made contemporary.

Exposed steel struts across the window wall, however, and the large and almost ridiculous roof combine with the ungainly outgrowths of organic-shaped balconies to add a quite different layer of potential meaning to the structure, as if this is a machine that is broken and has been jury-rigged back together. These inelegant accretions speak of compromise, pragmatism and fallibility.

Inside, the house is just good old-fashioned light and space. Rooms are nicely proportioned with pleasing contrasts between the large living room and other smaller rooms. Finishes are deftly handled, once again in series of contrasts: between, for example, a central core within the structure that is wrapped in anodised aluminium and the raw concrete of the bathrooms.

Oakland Hills

ADDRESS 43 Perth Place, Oakland 94705 [SF/A/CC Alameda 4 E2]
CLIENTS Lisa and David Shaw
STRUCTURAL ENGINEER Wes Ogawa
SIZE 4000 square feet (370 square metres)
ACCESS none

Philip Banta Architecture 1994

Oakland Hills

Fleisig House

The house is set so close to a water tower on the crest of a hill that, from a distance, the two seem linked. The large drum of the tower looms over the simple gable of the stucco house and adds an enigmatic twist to the design. Finding out that the tower is quite separate to the house is a disappointment that the architect goes some way to diminishing with an enigmatic feature of his own. This is a chimney stack that rises beside a roof terrace and is angled and notched in a way that makes its function not immediately obvious. More like a cubist bell tower than a chimney, it is not too far removed from Ricardo Logretta's campanile in Pershing Square, Los Angeles.

The basis of the design was to have a straightfoward box holding the core functions of the building such as the kitchens and bedrooms. To this was added a garage and office element with a steeply sloping roof and a colonnaded entryway. A small library tower was also appended, as was the larger volume of the living room with terrace and chimney above. The space between these add-ons forms an enclosed courtyard.

Oakland Hills

ADDRESS 1060 Amito Drive, Oakland 94705 [SF/A/CC Alameda 4 E1
CLIENTS David and Sara Fleisig
STRUCTURAL ENGINEER Juri Komendant
SIZE 2900 square feet (270 square metres)
ACCESS none

Gary Parsons 1993

Gary Parsons 1993

Besito Avenue House

Like so many hillside houses, this building has two quite different aspects when it comes to its street and canyon elevations, although it is even more schizophrenic than most. The street side reveals a modest, one-storey, barrel-vaulted volume, given a great sense of lightness and movement by the curved line of the eave. On the canyon side, however, the fluid and graceful Nissen hut becomes a swaggering battleship of perforated steel awnings, curved balconies and angled sections that plunge vertiginously five levels down to one of the hills' rare swimming pools. Rather than being offensive, however, the assurance of the design carries the day.

A minor construction miracle, the structure needed a total of 65 concrete piers to ensure that it and the pool did not end up at the bottom of the hill. This rugged engineering expresses itself throughout the house with exposed steel beams rising to support curved steel roof trusses.

The double-height living room has been particularly tailored to the needs of its musical occupants with an acoustical metal ceiling and a balcony for a baby grand piano and cello.

ADDRESS 1126 Besito Avenue, Oakland 94705 [SF/A/CC Alameda 6 A1]
STRUCTURAL ENGINEER Ingraham-DeJesse & Associates
SIZE 4000 square feet (370 square metres)
ACCESS none

Oakland Hills

Burks Toma 1993

House on Drury Road

As with his project on Alpine Terrace (see page 276), Mark Horton combines simple geometric forms with the use of cement board for this house. A circular concrete retaining wall supports the house on its ridge-top site and prepares one for an equally ascetic design. In this case, however, the project is softened considerably by the inclusion of a reassuringly familiar slate roof on a much smaller structure. There is a decidedly homely and comfortable feel to the building which belies the tough materials used.

ADDRESS 10 Drury Road, Oakland 94704
[SF/A/CC Alameda 6 A1]
CLIENT Eleanor Steffen
STRUCTURAL ENGINEER Lea & Sung
SIZE 2050 square feet (190 square metres)
ACCESS none

Oakland Hills

Mark Horton Architecture 1994

Oakland Hills

Mark Horton Architecture 1994

Becker House

Unrelentingly modern, the Becker House distains any comforting iconography. It is what it is: two boxes, one clad in corrugated aluminium, the other in cement board. So pure are their forms that not even guttering is allowed to intrude. Between these two Platonic shapes, a wall of etched glass suggests an undefined union.

The larger (cement) box contains the main living areas. One enters directly into the open-plan kitchen-dining-living room. So sleek and sophisticated is the kitchen, however, that its function is not immediately apparent. The appliances are grouped together in modules that lie flush with the internal walls and that express themselves as appended boxes on the exterior. The effect is of fitted cabinetry. A dark jarrah wood floor unites the space and a 12-foot-high ceiling seems to float above you. Below this level is the main bedroom, accessed via a freestanding stairway behind an etched glass wall.

The space between the two volumes is open except for a deck at street level and a corridor at the lower level. The metal box contains a garage and studio with a pair of additional bedrooms below.

The bridging deck provides spectacular views protected from the high winds that often buffet the hillside houses, and below it broad steps down to the garden create a natural theatre space.

Oakland Hills

ADDRESS 119 Strathmore Drive, Oakland [SF/A/CC Alameda 6 A1]
CLIENT Leslie Becker
STRUCTURAL ENGINEER Sear Brown
SIZE 2200 square feet (200 square metres)
ACCESS none

Jim Jennings Arkhitekture 1994

Jim Jennings Arkhitekture 1994

Hammonds House

One of the paradoxes of hillside living is that houses occupying some of the most beautiful land in cities such as Oakland and Los Angeles are often almost completely isolated from that land. They cling precariously to plummeting hillsides on spindly legs, or squat like castle keeps on their craggy plots. They usually have breathtaking views but they lack any genuine connection to the soil.

For this house, on a particularly steep and narrow site, the architects wanted to engage the elements by way of creating a garden and a court-yard. To do this they stepped the living quarters down the hillside, behind the garage, instead of following the common pattern of elevating every-thing high above ground level. This allowed the lower sections of the structure to connect to a garden. More surprisingly, a courtyard, enclosed only on three sides, has been located in the centre of the structure, between the principal volumes of the garage and the main living room, providing an unexpected and large open space which in turn makes the rooms that look on to it seem much bigger. These spaces are full of angles and surprising orientations and are handled in a notably sculptural way that denies their relatively modest size.

(Visitors to SF MOMA's show on William Wurster will realise that there are certain similarities with Wurster's Grover House of 1939 in the way the courtyard space is created.)

ADDRESS 7036 Norfolk Drive, Oakland 94705 [SF/A/CC Alameda 6 A2]
CLIENTS Glenn and Ann Hammonds
STRUCTURAL ENGINEER Dominic Chu
SIZE 2800 square feet (260 square metres)
ACCESS none

Oakland Hills

Cotten Residence

This house, designed for an enthusiastic horn player by architects who are quite capable of inducing apoplexy, has already raised an eyebrow or two. Inspired by the remains of a Selmar saxophone that were found in the ruins of the old house, destroyed in the Oakland blaze, the house is notable for the two golden, flared towers that rise like the brass section of a jazz band and the curved walls of a chimney that bears more than a passing resemblance to a saxophone. In the architects' words: '... this house includes a variety of musical strategies and motifs including stair towers and a fireplace rendered as horns. The house begins pianissimo at the street and builds to a fortissimo crescendo, as it cascades down the hill. The colors of the house are a range of the blues'.

Locals have a somewhat different take on the building and have nick-named it 'Three Mile Island', no doubt because glazed bubbles top off the twin towers and emit eerie beams of light at night.

Equally flamboyant inside, the practical elements of the structure – bedrooms, bathrooms, etc – are grouped around the huge chasm of a 30-foot-high open space.

Idiosyncratic to the maximum, this house might have been more at home in Los Angeles, but as a physical manifestation of someone's will, it is no different to the Spanish haciendas or tasteful moderns that have started to cover the fire zone.

ADDRESS 1985 Tunnel Road, Oakland 94705 [SF/A/CC Alameda 6 B2]
CLIENTS Henry and Leilani Cotten
STRUCTURAL ENGINEER Santos & Urrutia
SIZE 5000 square feet (465 square metres)
ACCESS none

Oakland Hills

Ace Architects 1994

Schmid Residence

The owner of this house gave two requirements to his architects, the first being that the house should be as fireproof as possible. The second was that it should be a simple box 'whose materials, proportions, elements and connections be honestly expressed and repeated throughout the building'. Working from an initial sketch by Beat Ernst, a Swiss-based architect, the Swiss-born project architect Jan Fillinger developed the concept in conjunction with his Swiss client. It is perhaps not surprising that the design is spartan, functional and meticulously executed.

The structure is a grid of galvanised steel columns and beams based on an 11-foot-wide by 10-foot-high module that is expressed throughout the structure. Cement board fills the grid. The street elevation is three bays wide by two high. The house is 66 feet long and increases to three floors on the downhill side of the plot. Floors are of concrete over corrugated steel panels, faced with acoustical sheet metal that forms the ceiling of the room below. An inverted suspension bridge leads from the sidewalk to the entrance.

The spare interiors are used as a backdrop to the owner's art collection but the house is not without its own moments of theatre. A shower in the main bedroom takes the form of a free-standing glass box, for example, and the garden of agave, iceplants, cacti and grasses promises to set this spartan box off to advantage.

Oakland Hills

ADDRESS 6365 Fairlane Drive, Oakland 94611 [SF/A/CC Alameda 6 B5]
CLIENT Frederick Schmid
STRUCTURAL ENGINEER Steven Tipping & Associates
SIZE 5280 square feet (490 square metres)
ACCESS none

Savidge Warren Fillinger 1993

Oakland Hills

Savidge Warren Fillinger 1993

Broadway Terrace House

Bernard Maybeck's elephantine Hearst Hall, built in 1899 and destroyed by fire in 1922, has been recreated in spirit in this Oakland house, itself a replacement for a structure lost in the fire of 1991.

The Broadway Terrace House is a petite 1400 square feet and, constructed primarily of chipboard, copper-clad asphalt shingles and stucco, it might seem an unlikely, or at least very faint, reflection of Hearst Hall. However, it is surprising how well it evokes the larger building.

The 22-foot-high ribs that support the vaulted ceiling of the living space are made from two by fours covered with oriented-strand board but the low-cost materials are given vibrant colours inspired by a design that Julia Morgan, a pupil of Maybeck, made for William Randolph Hearst's San Simeon.

To its credit, this building seems to be the people's choice as the strangest new house in the fire zone, although the same architects' Cotten House must also be a contender.

Oakland Hills

ADDRESS 6356 Broadway Terrace, Oakland 94607
[SF/A/CC Alameda 4 E5]
CLIENT Dixie Jordan
STRUCTURAL ENGINEER Santos & Urrutia
SIZE 1400 square feet (130 square metres)
ACCESS none

Ace Architects 1994

Langmaid House

These architects, not surprisingly given the name fate has bestowed on them, specialise in residential projects. In this design they have taken the idiom of the suburban home and gone some way toward deconstructing it. They have done this, however, without the slightest hint of irony and have, therefore, created a composition that is relatively complex without being threatening or difficult.

The plan reveals a simple rectangular form that has been rotated around an axis. A stuccoed two-storey volume aligns with this axis as does a gabled element, while a single-storey volume, wood-clad and pitched roofed in reference to the Bay's Craftsman tradition, has been located at approximately 60° to it. The rotation is expressed in plan by a semi-circular element that links the other masses. Internally, this creates a number of interconnected spaces branching out from a central core.

From the street, the house presents itself as a grouping of autonomous elements brought together almost capriciously. The familiarity of the materials, however, and of the basic language make it a recognisable variant of the suburban home and a comfortable presence.

Oakland Hills

ADDRESS 6308 Acacia Avenue,
Oakland 94618 [SF/A/ CC Alameda 4 E4]
CLIENTS Stephen and Sheila Langmaid
STRUCTURAL ENGINEER Dominic Chu
SIZE 4200 square feet (390 square metres)
ACCESS none

House + House Architecture 1994

House + House Architecture 1994

House on Alpine Terrace

The architect has used the potential of cement board to create a composition of geometric formality. The structure is divided into two: a cube and a barrel-vaulted volume, each overlaid with a strict 4 x 4 foot grid of cement board, defined by aluminium strip. A linking element is clad in an aluminium-faced board, using the same grid, as are various balconies and a chimney stack. The graph paper quality of the design makes the large volumes appear to be distilled to their essence, while even subtle variations from the rigidity of the grid – such as the angled balconies – attain eye-catching prominence.

The quality of construction is already apparent – and is a necessary precondition for the success of a project such as this.

ADDRESS 140 Alpine Terrace,
Oakland 94705 or 94618
[SF/A/CC Alameda 4 E4]
CLIENT Reesa Tansey and Gary Greenfield
STRUCTURAL ENGINEER Structural Design
Engineers
SIZE 4500 square feet (420 square metres)
ACCESS none

Oakland Hills

Mark Horton Architecture 1995

Oakland Hills

Mark Horton Architecture 1995

McLane Residence

This house is part racing yacht, part ark. Its footprint is a knife blade. Cold materials such as metal and glass have been used in ways that both maintain their toughness but also imbue them with an unexpectedly tactile quality. The sharp prow of the structure extends into the site, pointing over the hillcrest toward the Bay (or, unfortunately, and more accurately, toward another house). One side of the building bellys out into a curve and is clad in stucco. The other side has panels of corrugated aluminium that are arranged in a patchwork to catch the sun in different ways. A stark white interior is softened by a voluptuously curving gallery that overlooks the space.

The interplay of materials and the contrasts that arise are handled with assurance and the novelty of the form is striking.

Oakland Hills

ADDRESS 6131 Ocean View Drive, Oakland 94705 [SF/A/CC Alameda 4 E4]
CLIENTS Rob McLane and Merrily Look
STRUCTURAL ENGINEER Santos & Urrutia
SIZE 2300 square feet (215 square metres)
ACCESS none

Stanley Saitowitz 1994

Marin

Latrines, Headlands Center for the Arts

The Headlands Center for the Arts is a collection of old army buildings set amongst 12,000 acres of windswept hillside just over the Golden Gate Bridge in Marin. Occupied by the army for more than 100 years, the National Park Service took over the land in 1972 and subsequently invited a number of not-for-profit organisations to rehabilitate and use the various buildings.

The Headlands Center is based in Building 944, a barracks that dates back to 1907. David Ireland, an artist who has influenced architects such as Frank Gehry, oversaw the renovation of the public spaces in 944. He also collaborated with architect Mark Mack in the design of the Center's furniture. Ann Hamilton worked on the kitchens and mess hall and Bruce Tomb and John Randolph of the Interim Office of Architecture were responsible for the latrines.

Making no concessions to the new occupants of the building, Tomb and Randolph did not attempt to provide separate facilites for men and women or to soften the utilitarian nature of the original lavatories and showers.

Existing urinals, wcs and showers were all left in place but the rooms they occupy were stripped back to their bare bones. Walls were taken back to the point where the ghost-image of an old painted dado line is visible. New concrete work is rough-finished and the raw concrete floor is left exposed. The urinals were disconnected but left, marching in place, along one wall, while the wcs were given oversized and unconventional plumbing that snakes down from the ceiling and were surrounded by new sensuously curving but darkly threatening stalls of heavy sheet steel. More like animal pens than anything designed for human use, they provide the minimum of privacy and evoke disquieting images of stockyards, gas chambers and the Francis Bacon work, *Triptych – May-June* 1973.

Marin

Interim Office of Architecture 1987

Marin

Interim Office of Architecture 1987

The showers are equally unrelenting in the way that they obliterate any notions of individuality and deny differences between the sexes. Like the rooms themselves, one feels that the people who use these facilities will be stripped back to their essence.

ADDRESS 944 Fort Barry, Sausalito 94965[GG Marin G]
The Thomas Guide provides the most rudimentary map for this section of the Marin peninsula. Approaching from the south, take the Alexander Exit off Highway 101 North, just after the Golden Gate Bridge, and turn left immediately, going under the highway. Turn right on to Conzelman Road, just before the entrance to Golden Gate Bridge. Then follow signs. From the north, take Highway 101 South to the fourth Sausalito exit, the last exit before the Golden Gate Bridge. Turn left at stop sign then immediately right on to Conzelman Road. Follow signs. Directions: call 415 331 2887
CLIENT Headlands Center for the Arts
SIZE 1100 square feet (100 square metres)
ACCESS call 415 331 2787

Interim Office of Architecture 1987

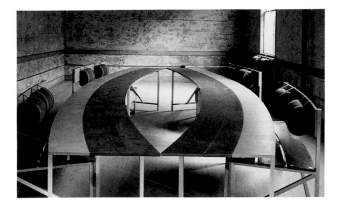

Marin

Interim Office of Architecture 1987

Larkspur Fire Station Number 2

Despite a very functional programme, the architects have attempted to highlight the natural drama of a fire station and to create moments of theatre for passers-by. Not only are the garage doors completely glazed, but also the tower that contains the firemen's pole. This most iconic element, usually unseen, has been given a literally pivotal position with its tower linking the garage to the administrative areas and crew quarters. More obvious iconography – the flag – has been incorporated into an eyebrow that extends over the garage doors in an historical reference to Californian firestations of the 1950s (some of the state's most successful civic architecture).

Materials are rudimentary – concrete block, stucco and sheet metal – but the forms are enlivened by odd angles and by incisions cut into the volume of the administration block to create colonnades and balconies.

ADDRESS 15 Barry Way, Larkspur 94939 [GG Marin 10D D4]
CLIENT City of Larkspur
STRUCTURAL ENGINEER HKA
CONTRACT VALUE $1.1 million
SIZE 6200 square feet (576 square metres)
ACCESS none

Marin

Allied Architects 1991

Allied Architects 1991

Luchetti House

Although the architect has described the asymmetrically curved roof of this house as 'a loaf of bread' it is not a metaphor that survives for long, since it is a delicate construction characterised by the architect's lightness of touch. What the building actually alludes to in its structure is the world of yachting. The 'loaf' is a 65 feet long by 22.5 feet high vaulted volume that faces the Bay at Sausalito. Within it, slender, tapering steel columns – so like masts that it makes no difference – support asymmetrical bowstring trusses, over which the curve of the roof seems to have been pulled taut like fabric. Steel cables designed to stabilise the overhang of the roof during high winds extend from the tip of each truss and are secured at ground level. The southern elevation comprises a window wall made up of large panes of glass supported by thin, steel mullions that hardly catch one's eye.

Like a sailing boat, the structure of the house seems to rely on the opposition of forces for its integrity. Like a sailing boat, its dynamism comes from the perception that it is harnessing and directing natural forces.

ADDRESS 507 Sausalito Boulevard, Sausalito 94965 [GG Marin 14 A5]
CLIENTS Peter and Emily Luchetti
STRUCTURAL ENGINEER Charles Chaloff Consulting Engineers
SIZE 2800 square feet (260 square metres)
ACCESS none

Marin

Robert Luchetti Associates 1991

Point Tiburon

Tiburon must occupy one of the most beautiful locations in the Bay area and it is, therefore, no surprise that the consultation and planning procedures involved in the creation of this mixed residential and commercial development were time consuming and that it took ten years to complete the project. What is surprising is that Point Tiburon should be the end result.

On the plus side, the architecture is a largely very pleasant Bay Area Modern, some of it quite sculptural, all of it obviously thoughtfully designed. There are gardens, swimming pools, parking lots, there is even a lagoon. Between the Bay-side leg of the development and the water's edge there is a public space in the form of a broad sward of grass. Of the 155 condominium units, 20 are below market rate. Overall there is the feeling that a great deal of sensitive thought has gone into the design.

On the negative side, you could list almost all of the above. There is the unnerving feeling that this is a seriously misguided project and that it could quite easily – and more suitably – be picked up and put down next to a golf course in Scottsdale, Arizona. The development is too big, it is unrelentingly suburban, its relationship to its spectacular site and the older part of the town is anything but visceral and the whole thing radiates a frightening air of immutability.

One only has to walk through the town to Beach Road with its views of Belvedere Cove to realise that a model for development in Tiburon already existed in the chaotic cascade of houses that line the Cove. Point Tiburon is Valium World. The possibility of creating streets, squares, promenades and a mix of housing types and styles, not to mention a genuine mix of income levels, that would have the possibility of future change and growth has been exchanged for an anodyne 'planned development' that has sucked the life out of the town.

Fisher-Friedman Associates 1986

Marin

Fisher-Friedman Associates 1986

It should be noted, however, that this project has won numerous awards and one must assume that the lengthy consultation processes produced some sort of consensus. But Point Tiburon's existence is still something of a mystery: who wanted it and what alternatives were offered?

ADDRESS Tiburon Boulevard and Main Street, Tiburon 94920 [GG Marin 14 D2]
CLIENT Innisfree Company
STRUCTURAL ENGINEER Robinson Meier Juilly
CONTRACT VALUE $30 million
SIZE 272,288 square feet (25,300 square metres)
ACCESS retail segment open

Fisher-Friedman Associates 1986

Marin

Fisher-Friedman Associates 1986

Index

San Francisco: a guide to recent architecture

San Francisco: a guide to recent architecture

San Francisco: a guide to recent architecture

San Francisco: a guide to recent architecture

San Francisco: a guide to recent architecture

San Francisco: a guide to recent architecture

San Francisco: a guide to recent architecture